IMPORTANT SITES FOR BIRDS
IN THE
CHANNEL ISLANDS

INCLUDING RECOGNISED
IMPORTANT BIRD AREAS

ISBN 0 951 8075 7 9

Cover illustration: Nick Parlett
Other illustrations: Will Woodrow, © Ian Buxton.

© La Société Guernesiaise 1997

Published by La Société Guernesiaise, Candie Gardens, St Peter Port,
Guernsey GY1 1UG

in conjunction with:

The Société Jersiaise, 7 Pier Road, St Helier, Jersey JE2 4XW
The States of Guernsey Board of Administration, Sir Charles Frossard House,
La Charroterie, St Peter Port, Guernsey GY1 1FH
Environment & Countryside Services, The States of Jersey Planning and Environment
Committee, States Offices, South Hill, St Helier, Jersey JE2 4US
and
The Royal Society for the Protection of Birds, The Lodge, Sandy,
Bedfordshire, SG19 2DL

Important Sites for Birds in the Channel Islands
Including Recognised Important Bird Areas

Edited by Paul K.Veron

This book should be cited as: P. K.Veron (Ed.) 1997 *Important Sites for Birds in the Channel Islands.* La Société Guernesiaise.

Contents

Foreword by Julian Pettifer, President of the Royal Society for the Protection of Birds

Today nature conservation enjoys the respect and support of a larger part of the community than ever before. Despite this goodwill, both the countryside, the marine environment and the wildlife they support still suffer from changes in management, over-exploitation and neglect. This book helps to advance nature conservation on the Channel Islands by identifying the most important areas for birds.

The rich variety of birds on the Channel Islands has long been recognised by local enthusiasts and visiting birdwatchers. Recently some of the islands' favourite birds have been celebrated and promoted in publicity aimed at attracting more visitors to the islands. The islands' special environment and unique ecology is at last recognised as one of the Channel Islands' greatest assets.

This book is a result of a true partnership, involving amateur birdwatchers coordinated by La Société Guernesiaise and the Société Jersiaise, a conservation organisation – the Royal Society for the Protection of Birds and the two principal governing bodies of the islands – the States of Guernsey and the States of Jersey. This collaboration has resulted in an important book that will play a substantive role in conserving the islands' birdlife, thus contributing to the conservation of the Channel Islands' biodiversity.

Julian Pettifer.

1997.

Foreword by Roger Long, Past President of the Société Jersiaise, and Nigel Jee, Past President of La Société Guernesiaise and Past Chairman of The National Trust of Guernsey.

Islands have always held a fascination for naturalists. Every island is to some extent unique, with a geology, climate, fauna and flora of its own. Until comparatively recently in geological time the Channel Islands were part of continental Europe, and their animals and plants are still mainly continental species. A few, such as the Jersey bank-vole and Guernsey vole, have been isolated for long enough to develop recognisable differences from their relatives elsewhere, but the islands lack the large number of endemics that have evolved in remote island groups like the Galapagos, which have never been joined to a land-mass.

The Channel Islands do, however, have an extremely rich flora and fauna. This is largely due to the wide variety of habitats, both natural and man-made, contained within a small area. Even within an island as small as Herm, the calcareous dunes of the north support a totally different set of species from the acid cliff-top heathland of the south, and the agricultural land and the abandoned quarries provide yet more habitats.

Other factors that contribute to the diversity of life in the islands are the mild Atlantic climate, the extremely wide tidal range, and the islands' position on the migration routes of birds and insects up and down the western fringe of Europe.

Within the Channel Islands, the natural differences between the islands have been further widened by differing histories of land management. Windswept Alderney, with its central settlement surrounded by open fields, is totally different from Jersey, with its scattered farmsteads and fields enclosed by high hedgebanks and its numerous inland valleys. Sark, though closer in size to Alderney, takes its landscape from Jersey, from where it was colonised in the 16th century.

Guernsey is similar to Jersey in having scattered settlements and fields enclosed by hedgebanks, but on to this landscape has been superimposed a legacy of abandoned quarries in the north, and an intensive horticultural industry which involved the whole island. Many of the glasshouses have gone, but the houses and packing sheds that went with them remain scattered over the landscape. To this must be added the new housing that has been necessary to accommodate a growing population in all the main islands.

With the demands on land for development and recreation becoming ever more intense, it has become essential to identify those sites that are of particular importance to wildlife, to define their boundaries and to take steps to ensure their conservation.

Birds are excellent indicators of the biological health and richness of a habitat. An area which has plenty of birds will almost certainly have a rich flora and a wide diversity of insects and other groups of animals. Reading through the list of important sites for birds described in this book, one cannot help concluding that they are all sites worthy of conservation, not only for the sake of birds, but also for other animals and the plants that they contain.

We commend the book to all birdwatchers, decision-makers, and everyone with an interest in the natural history of the Channel Islands.

1997.

Preface

by John Waldon, Regional Officer (South-west), RSPB

The birds on the Channel Islands make an important contribution to Europe's wildlife. The islands provide essential habitats for an impressive range and variety of birds including species that rely on the islands during their extensive migrations. A further group of birds, the seabirds, return from ocean wanderings to nest on the rocky islands, shores and cliffs. In winter the islands and coastal waters support a different assemblage of birds. On the intertidal rocky shores flocks of turnstones reach numbers of international importance during migration and in winter, and feed alongside ringed plovers and wildfowl, while in nearshore waters divers and grebes regularly occur. It is this impressive variety of birdlife that requires conservation action if it is to be sustained.

Many of the birds rely on special sites which are identified in this book. Some of these species are in decline throughout Europe and protection of their key sites will be an essential step towards conserving these birds and so maintaining a part of the islands' biodiversity. This book identifies the prime sites for birds on the islands.

In 1989 *Important Bird Areas in Europe* was published (ICBP Technical Publication No 9), followed in 1992 by *Important Bird Areas in the UK, including the Channel Islands and the Isle of Man*. Both identified the importance of the Channel Islands.

Important Bird areas (IBAs) are sites recognised as being important and designated as such in the books mentioned above. They include sites qualifying for designation as Special Protection Areas under European Community Directive 79/409 on the Conservation of Wild Birds. Some of these would also be candidates for designation as Wetlands of international Importance under the Ramsar Convention.

There are also sites of importance for birds that fail to meet the criteria for designation as IBAs. Such sites play an essential role in supporting birds and are for the first time identified throughout the islands. This inventory is offered to enable protection and enhancement to be provided to the important semi-natural habitats.

Besides the ecological arguments for protecting these sites, there is another reason for identifying the best places for birds. Birdwatching today is an enormously popular pastime. The pursuit of eco-tourism or 'green' tourism requires that the environment be maintained so that the very resource that attracts people is protected and suitably exploited.

The protection of these sites and the birds they support is essential if the islands' biodiversity is to be maintained. It is rich and varied and deserves recognition as the first step towards ensuring the Channel Islands' bird life remains to be appreciated in the future. This is a challenge requiring in some cases new legislation and positive land management.

ACKNOWLEDGEMENTS

This book would never have been produced without the commitment and support of all the organisations (government and voluntary) mentioned on the title page. This joint venture bodes well for the future of the important sites for birds in the Channel Islands.

The project was overseen from the outset by a small working group, comprised of the following people in addition to the editor, Dr Michael Romeril, Mike Stentiford, Mick Dryden, Griff Caldwell, Ian McEwan and John Waldon.

The main authors of the book are Mick Dryden and Ian Buxton (Jersey), Julian Medland and Griff Caldwell (Guernsey), Paul Veron and Griff Caldwell (Alderney, Sark, Herm, Jethou and Offshore Islets) and John Waldon (international conventions and legislation). To them everyone involved in this project is very grateful. Griff Caldwell provided support to see this project through, while Joan Bagley and Barry Wells turned the various texts into the finished article.

Finally the work of hundreds of amateur naturalists and bird-watchers must be acknowledged. Without their assiduous and often arduous work such a publication would surely not be possible. They have, each of them, made the most important contribution of all - establishing the base from which we can conserve and enhance our environment for ourselves and for our children.

Paul K. Veron
1997

International Conventions and UK Legislation for Wildlife Protection

The Channel Islands lie within the Gulf of St Malo and in places are less than 12 km from the coast of Normandy. The close proximity to the continent of Europe is reflected within the islands' flora and fauna. In particular, the ability of birds to cross water with apparent ease continually reminds us of this link. The Channel Islands' resident birds are augmented during periods of migration, during the nesting season when, in addition to the passerine summer visitors, thousands of seabirds nest on the islands' cliffs and rock islets, and during hard weather movements of birds in the period when they are escaping frozen conditions on the Continent and in Britain.

Today nature conservation calls for protection to be afforded to birds throughout their range and during their extraordinary migrations. While protection of vulnerable, rare and common species is essential, such protection will achieve little if the habitats required by these birds are not also protected.

In the UK habitat protection is provided by an array of legislation, some originating in the UK and others with origins in what is now the European Union (EU). A brief review of this 'international' legislation is provided to explain the relevance of certain designations and to clarify the status of species in Europe and the UK.

The Channel Islands are not part of the UK but are dependencies of the British Crown. Jersey and Guernsey are not members of the European Union; instead they enjoy a 'special relationship' with the EU arising from Article 227 (5) of the EEC Treaty and Protocol No. 3 to the Treaty of Accession.

International wildlife conventions ratified by the UK Government on behalf of both the States of Guernsey and Jersey are the 'Bonn' Convention on the Conservation of Migratory Species of Wild Animals and the 'Washington' Convention on International Trade in Endangered Species of Fauna and Flora (CITES). In addition, the UK Government has, on behalf of Jersey, ratified the 'Ramsar' Convention on Wetlands of International Importance. The States of Guernsey have recently agreed to request the UK Government to ratify this Convention on their behalf.

The Bonn Convention on the Conservation of Migratory Species of Wild Animals requires the protection of endangered migratory species and encourages separate international agreements covering particular species. Such an agreement is the Pan African-Eurasian Waterbird Agreement.

The CITES Convention which was signed in 1974 in Washington, USA, prohibits or regulates international trade in species which are threatened with extinction or are likely to become so, and which are subject to significant trade.

The Ramsar Convention seeks the conservation of wetlands, particularly those of importance for waterfowl. The Convention defines wetlands as including marsh and open water, whether natural or artificial, permanent or temporary, fresh or salt and including areas of sea, the depth of which at low tide does not exceed six metres. Article 2 requires each Contracting Party to list wetlands of international importance. Article 3 promotes the 'wise use' of wetlands. To date part of the south-east shoreline of Jersey has been identified as meeting the criteria for designation, and it is likely that other shorelines in the Channel Islands are of sufficient importance to qualify.

The conservation of natural habitats throughout Europe is an essential part of the EU's ongoing environmental strategy. The EU's 5th Environment Programme aims to maintain biodiversity through sustainable land management in and around habitats of importance. A coherent network of such sites, referred to as Natura 2000, is proposed. This will combine Special Protection Areas (SPAs) arising from The Birds Directive, with Special Areas of Conservation (SACs) that originate from The Habitats and Species Directive. This network will complement the control in the trade in wild species provided by the CITES Convention and the protection of species by other measures.

The maintenance and restoration of Europe's flora and fauna within Natura 2000 in the wider countryside is sought by the EU's Habitats and Species Directive 92/43/EEC and the Directive on The Conservation of Wild Birds 79/409/EEC. In Great Britain these sites and Directives are delivered in part by the Wildlife and Countryside Act 1981 (amended in 1985). This Act provides for the protection of nationally important sites by notification as Sites of Special Scientific Interest (SSSI). It also makes it an offence to kill wild birds (exceptions include quarry species).

In the UK SSSIs are widely considered to be the cornerstone of nature conservation. The network of SSSIs seeks to conserve the variety and geographical range of plant and animal communities. Two important principles underlie the selection of SSSI: the exemplary site principle used for the best examples of habitats and the species they support, and the minimum standards principle which applies chiefly to species populations.

Within the Council of Europe, the 'Berne' Convention on the Conservation of European Wildlife and Natural Habitats imposes obligations to conserve wild plants, birds and other animals with particular emphasis on endangered and vulnerable species and their habitats. The provisions of the Convention are echoed in the EC Birds Directive as well as the UK's wildlife legislation. The Convention has been ratified on behalf of Jersey, but full involvement will follow only when the proposed new Jersey Wildlife Law (currently well advanced) is implemented.

The concept of sustainable development or sustainability was given public prominence following the Earth Summit in Rio de Janerio in 1992. At the Rio Conference, the maintenance of biodiversity was deemed a critical aspect of successful sustainable development and the Convention on Biological Diversity was an important product of the Earth Summit. It was signed in Rio by 153 countries including the UK and the

European Community and came into force in December 1996. Jersey was included in the UK ratification of the Convention. Article 6A of the Convention requires each contracting party to:

'develop national strategies, plans or programmes for the conservation and sustainable use of biological diversity, or adapt for this purpose existing strategies, plans or programmes which shall reflect, inter alia, the measures set out in the Convention.'

The UK Government produced its own Action Plan in January 1994 and established the Biodiversity Steering Group to set targets for species and habitats. Government endorsement was given in May 1996 (CM3260) to the Steering Group's report to the planning process, including species and habitat action plans.

Jersey's Biodiversity Plan (first draft) was produced in 1993. Modifications to produce the final Strategy document have, unfortunately, taken longer than expected. The 1996 Annual Report to the States of Jersey from the Environmental Adviser says of the Strategy "Its completion and implementation must be a high priority."

Guernsey is progressing a similar initiative, but is at a less advanced stage in its development.

Guide to the Inventory

INTRODUCTION

This section helps to interpret the site accounts which form the main part of this book. The geographical area of the whole of the Channel Islands, including the full territories of both the Bailiwick of Guernsey and the Bailiwick of Jersey, are covered in this publication.

MAPS

Location maps are included in pages 13 to 17. These maps do not show definitive boundaries for each area. There are separate maps for the Channel Islands and the Gulf of St. Malo; Jersey; Guernsey; Sark, Brecqhou, Herm, Jethou and offshore islets; and Alderney and offshore islets.

On each map recognised Important Bird Areas are shown either in black or by cross-shading. The latter applies only to the extensive coastal sites, thus enabling the line of the coast itself to remain distinguishable. Sites which do not qualify as recognised IBAs, but are otherwise important sites in a Channel Islands context are shown by use of open circles.

Against each site on the map is given that site's unique code reference: a two digit number followed by a letter indicating in which section of the site accounts the area will be found (e.g. G = Guernsey, J = Jersey). This enables cross-referencing to the list of sites and to the site accounts in the body of the text.

BOUNDARIES

Many of the sites included in this book do not have a finalised boundary. Indeed the maps included show the location of each area but do not define the boundaries. In some cases boundaries have been established, while in others further fieldwork will be necessary before they can be defined. In all cases decision-makers are encouraged to consult with the relevant Société, and in cases involving recognised Important Bird Areas the RSPB, should a proposal appear likely to affect in any way a site in this book. Decision-makers are further encouraged to adopt a precautionary approach.

THE SITE ACCOUNTS

The site accounts have been grouped into two categories.

a. Recognised Important Bird Areas.

These are sites recognised as being important and already designated as such in the book published by the RSPB "Important Bird Areas in the UK, including the Channel Islands an the Isle of Man".

b. Other sites which are deemed to be of Channel Islands importance for birds.

Reference to Sites of Special Importance (SSIs) in the Jersey site accounts relate to sites to be designated by the States of Jersey. They are not the same as Sites of Special Scientific Interest (SSSIs) in the UK, as the States of Jersey use their own criteria for site assessment.

The site description for each area covers the physiography and main habitat of the site including any special flora or fauna of interest (other than birds) if known.

A list of sites included in the book is given on pages 9 and 10. The sites have been numbered and listed in the order in which their description accounts appear in the body of the book.

Each site account is headed by the name of the area. Where alternative names exist in common usage these are included in parentheses. This is then followed by the approximate location of the site on the relevant Ordnance Survey sheet and its rough area measured in hectares (ha). There is also a short summary of the type of site involved and the key ornithological interest which gives rise to its inclusion in the book.

BIRD INFORMATION: DATA SOURCES USED

The bird data used in this book, both in selecting sites and in compiling the individual site accounts, has in the main been accumulated by fieldworkers operating under the auspices of La Société Guernesiaise and the Société Jersiaise. In many cases the data has been collected as part of a national project. Such data includes that submitted in connection with the following national surveys:

British Trust for Ornithology (BTO)/Wildfowl and Wetlands Trust (WWT)/Joint Nature Conservation Committee (JNCC)/Royal Society for the Protection of Birds (RSPB): Birds of Estuaries Enquiry and National Waterfowl Count Scheme (now Wetland Bird Survey).

JNCC/Seabird Group: Seabird Colony Register.

BTO/Wader Study Group (WSG): Winter Shorebird Counts.

Species-specific monitoring or survey programmes involving RSPB or NCC eg terns and cirl buntings.

BIRD INFORMATION: GUIDE TO INTERPRETING THE SITE ACCOUNTS

A summary of the main ornithological importance of each site is included in the section headed 'Birds'. This is a brief account only of the species occurring on a recognised IBA which are present in nationally or internationally important numbers. Other species which are of importance in a local context are also listed, and it is these which are detailed in the section headed 'Birds' for the sites of Channel Islands Importance. Where numbers are known accurately they are given. Bird species are referred to in the text by their common names, with a full list of scientific names given in Appendix 1.

CONSERVATION ISSUES

Although, for a number of sites, information is incomplete, an attempt has been made to identify any conservation issues which may be relevant to each site. This information is not definitive, nor is it static. The position will change with time. Reference is made not only to issues concerning negative 'threats' to sites, but also to where positive beneficial management steps are necessary.

UPDATING

The process of identifying and listing recognised Important Bird Areas and sites of Channel Islands importance is dynamic. Over time, and in some cases over a surprisingly short time, changes to land-use and/or species status and distribution will mean that the information, including which sites are identified and listed, will need to be updated. Any information which may be relevant in this context should be sent to La Société Guernesiaise or the Société Jersiaise (as appropriate).

MORE DETAILED INFORMATION

Should you require further information about any of the sites mentioned in this book, you are encouraged to contact La Société Guernesiaise (01481-725093) for sites within Guernsey, Alderney, Sark and Herm (including offshore islets and stacks), and the Société Jersiaise (01534-58314), or the States Ecologist, Environment & Countryside Services, Planning Department (01534-25511), for sites within Jersey (including Les Écréhous and Les Minquiers reefs).

ACCESS

The book describes areas in each of the Channel Islands. Some of these areas are in public ownership with open access, while others are in private ownership. Inclusion in the inventory must not be taken to imply rights of access.

REFERENCES

Cramp, S, Bourne, WRP and Saunders, D 1974. *The Seabirds of Britain and Ireland*. Collins, London.

Dobson, R & Lockley, RM 1946. Gannets breeding in the Channel Isles: two new colonies. *British Birds* 39: 309-312.

Hill, MG 1990. The Alderney gannetries - photographic counts of Ortac and Les Etacs, Channel Islands, 1979-1989. *Seabird* 12: 45-52.

Veron, PK 1979-1993. *Vale Marais Reports*. Private publication.

USEFUL READING

Bisson, AJ 1976. *A List of the Birds of Guernsey*. Guernsey.

Bisson, AJ 1989. *A List of the Birds of Guernsey Update: also checklist of Birds of the Channel Islands*. Guernsey.

Burrow, RVM 1974. A Brief History of the Storm Petrel on Burhou. *Seabird* 4: 49-54.

Buxton, IJ 1986. Winter Shorebirds in Jersey. *Annual Bulletin Société Jersiaise* 24: 265-269.

Buxton, IJ 1996. *Les Écréhous, Jersey*. Ornithology. 38-45.

Caldwell, FG 1996. A brief history of nature conservation in Guernsey. *La Société Guernesiaise Transactions* Vol. 23 Pt. 5 942-963.

Dobson, R 1952. *The Birds of the Channel Islands*. Staples Press, Newton Abbot.

Gilmour, J et al 1992. The Importance of Guernsey Quarries for Conservation. *La Société Guernesiaise Transactions* Vol. 23 Pt. 1 92-134.

Grimmett RFA & Jones, TA 1989. *Important Bird Areas in Europe*. Cambridge. ICBP.

Groupe Ornithologique Normand. 1991. *Atlas des Oiseaux Nicheurs de Normandie et des Iles Anglo-Normands*. Caen.

Hill, MG 1991. *The Distribution of Breeding Seabirds in The Bailiwick of Guernsey*, 1986-1990. La Société Guernesiaise.

Hill, MG 1994. *The Bailiwick Seabird Summary, 1994*. Unpublished Report. La Société Guernesiaise.

Hill, MG 1994. Manx Shearwaters, (Puffinus puffinus) Breeding in The Bailiwick of Guernsey, Channel Islands. *Seabird* 16: 41-45.

Hill, MG 1995. *The Fulmar (Fulmarus glacialis) In The Bailiwick of Guernsey, 1946-1994*. Unpublished Report. La Société Guernesiaise.

Land Use Consultants 1989. *A Strategy for the Conservation and Enhancement of Guernsey's Rural Environment*. Report for the States of Guernsey.

La Société Guernesiaise: Annual *Transactions*.

The Société Jersiaise: Annual *Bulletins*.

The Société Jersiaise: *Annual Jersey Bird Reports*, the Société Jersiaise 1991 onwards.

The Société Jersiaise 1972. *Birds in Jersey: a systematic list*.

Lloyd, CS, Tasker, ML & Partridge, KE 1991. *The Status of Seabirds Breeding in Britain and Ireland*. T & AD Poyser, Calton.

Long, R 1981. Review of Birds in the Channel Islands, 1951-1980. *British Birds* 74: 327-344.

Long, R 1995. Bird-ringing in the Channel Islands: the first fifty years. *The Société Jersiaise Bulletin*. 26(3) 381-388.

Mendham, ML 1990. *A List of the Birds of Alderney*. The Alderney Society, Alderney.

Milton, ND 1992. *The Status And Distribution Of Red Data Birds In The Channel Islands*. RSPB. South-west Region Office.

Pritchard, DE, Housden, SD, Mudge, GP, Galbraith, CA and Pienkowski, MW (Eds) 1992. *Important Bird Areas in the UK including the Channel Islands and the Isle of Man*. RSPB.

Rountree, FRG 1974. *Birds of Sark*. Sark Ornithological Committee, Sark.

Stentiford, M 1987. *The Birdwatchers' Jersey*. BBC Radio Jersey.

Tucker, GM & Heath, MF 1994. *Birds In Europe: Their Conservation Status*. Cambridge. Birdlife International.

Veron, PK 1989. Ornithology in the Channel Islands - One Man's Contribution. *La Société Guernesiaise Transactions* Vol. 22 Pt. 3 480-505.

Young, HJ, Dryden, M & Tonge, SJ 1996. Birds of the North Coast of Jersey. *The Société Jersiaise Bulletin*. 26 (4) 512-522.

LIST OF SITES

JERSEY

01J   Les Landes
02J   Crabbé
03J   La Tête de Frémont
04J   Les Platons / Egypt
05J   Les Hurets
06J   Le Jardin d'Olivet
07J   Noirmont
08J   Portelet Common
09J   Le Ouaisné Common
10J   La Lande du Ouest
11J   Le Beauport / Les Creux
12J   L'Étacq
13J   Le Mont Rossignol
14J   Le Mont à la Brune / Le Mont du Jubilé
15J   Petit Port
16J   Jersey Shoreline
17J   Les Écréhous
18J   Elizabeth Castle
19J   Le Hocq
20J   L'Étacquerel Fort (Bouley Bay)
21J   North Coast Cliffs
22J   Le Plateau des Minquiers
23J   South-west Cliffs
24J   La Mare au Seigneur (St Ouen's Pond)
25J   Grouville Marsh
26J   Longueville Marsh (Les Prés Dormant)
27J   Pont Marquet
28J   Les Quennevais / La Moye
29J   Gorey Common
30J   Wooded Inland Valleys

GUERNSEY

01G   Pleinmont
02G   L'Ancresse
03G   South Coast Cliffs
04G   Guernsey Shoreline
05G   Belle Greve Bay
06G   Grande Havre Bay

07G   Fort le Crocq
08G   Pulias Pond
09G   Vingtaine de l'Epine
10G   Vale Marais
11G   Vale Pond
12G   St Saviour's Reservoir
13G   La Grande Mare
14G   Les Landes, Vale
15G   L'Erée
16G   St Sampson's Marais
17G   Wooded Inland Valleys
18G   Lihou Island

ALDERNEY

01A   Le Giffoine
02A   Trois Vaux
03A   Les Étacs (The Garden Rocks)
04A   Ortac
05A   Alderney Mainland
06A   Burhou, Renonquet Reef and Les Casquets Rock

SARK

01S   Big Sark
02S   Little Sark (including L'Étac de Serk)
03S   Brecqhou

HERM, JETHOU and OFFSHORE ISLETS

01H   Herm and Offshore Islets
02H   Jethou
03H   Les Amfroques (The Humps)

SITE MAPS

THE CHANNEL ISLANDS IN THE GULF OF ST MALO

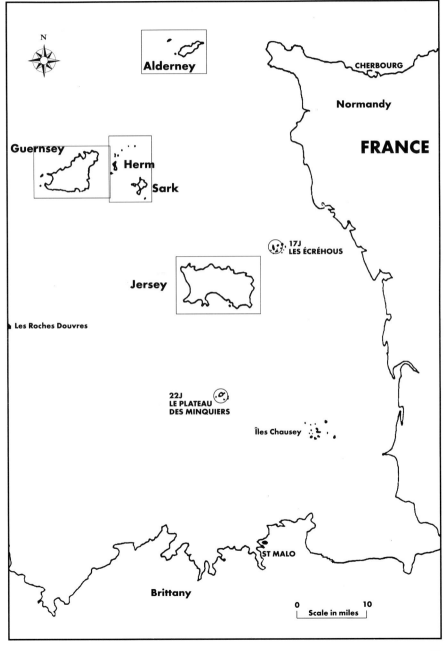

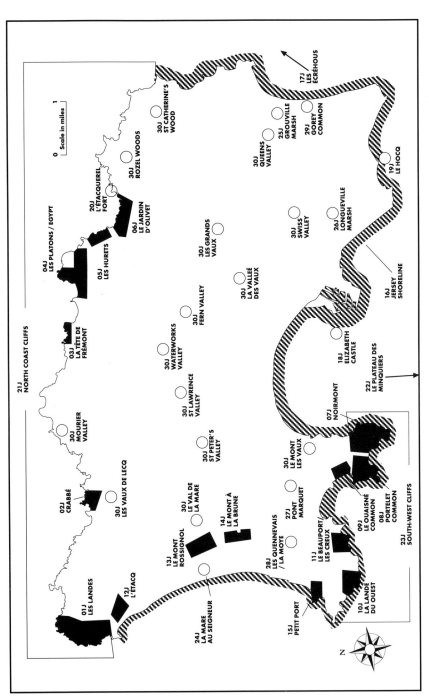

JERSEY

Scale in miles

21J
NORTH COAST CLIFFS

17J
LES
ÉCRÉHOUS

30J
ST CATHERINE'S
WOOD

30J
ROZEL WOODS

25J
GROUVILLE
MARSH

29J
GOREY
COMMON

30J
QUEENS
VALLEY

20J
L'ÉTACQUEREL
FORT

06J
LE JARDIN
D'OLIVET

04J
LES PLATONS / EGYPT

05J
LES HURETS

19J
LE HOCQ

30J
LES GRANDS
VAUX

30J
SWISS
VALLEY

26J
LONGUEVILLE
MARSH

03J
LA TÊTE DE
FRÉMONT

30J
LA VALLÉE
DES VAUX

30J
FERN VALLEY

16J
JERSEY
SHORELINE

30J
WATERWORKS
VALLEY

18J
ELIZABETH
CASTLE

22J
LE PLATEAU DES
MINQUIERS

30J
MOURIER
VALLEY

30J
ST LAWRENCE
VALLEY

07J
NOIRMONT

30J
ST PETER'S
VALLEY

30J
LE MONT
LES VAUX

02J
CRABBÉ

30J
LES VAUX DE LECQ

30J
LE VAL DE
LA MARE

14J
LE MONT À
LA BRUNE

27J
PONT
MARQUET

09J
LE OUAISNÉ
COMMON

08J
PORTELET
COMMON

23J
SOUTH-WEST CLIFFS

13J
LE MONT
ROSSIGNOL

28J
LES QUENNEVAIS
/ LA MOYE

11J
LE BEAUPORT/
LES CREUX

10J
LA LANDE
DU OUEST

01J
LES LANDES

12J
L'ÉTACQ

24J
LA MARE
AU SEIGNEUR

15J
PETIT PORT

N

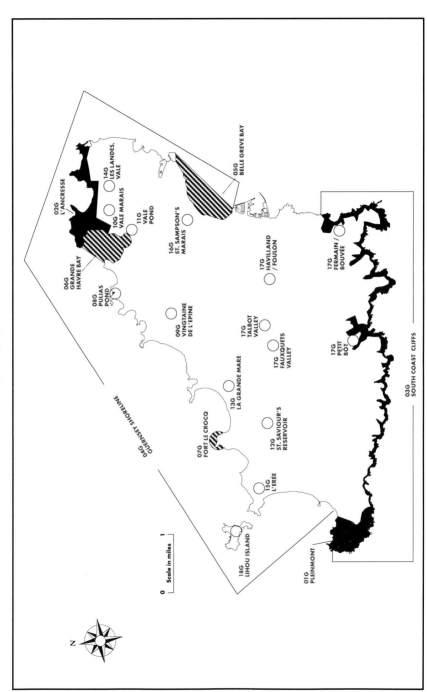

GUERNSEY

02G
L'ANCRESSE

14G
LES LANDES,
VALE

05G
BELLE GREVE BAY

10G
VALE MARAIS

11G
VALE
POND

16G
ST. SAMPSON'S
MARAIS

17G
HAVILLAND
/ FOULON

17G
FERMAIN /
BOUVÉE

06G
GRANDE
HAVRE BAY

08G
PULIAS
POND

09G
VINGTAINE
DE L'EPINE

17G
TALBOT
VALLEY

17G
FAUXQUETS
VALLEY

17G
PETIT
BOT

03G
SOUTH COAST CLIFFS

13G
LA GRANDE MARE

07G
FORT LE CROCQ

12G
ST. SAVIOUR'S
RESERVOIR

15G
L'ERÉE

04G
GUERNSEY SHORELINE

18G
LIHOU ISLAND

01G
PLEINMONT

Scale in miles

0   1

N

ALDERNEY AND OFFSHORE ISLETS

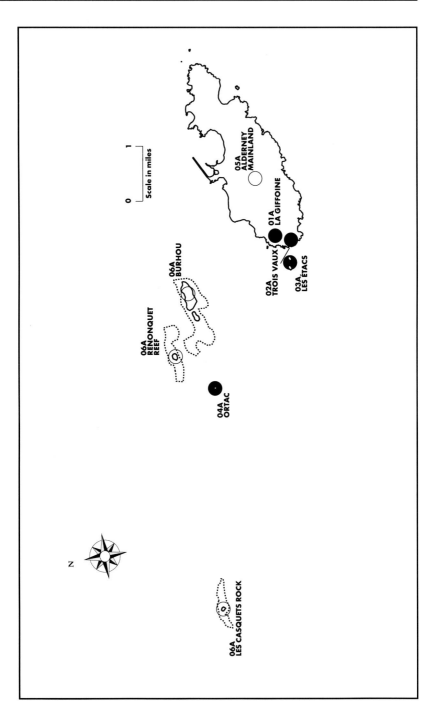

Scale in miles

0   1

N

05A
ALDERNEY
MAINLAND

01A
LA GIFFOINE

02A
TROIS VAUX

03A
LES ETACS

06A
BURHOU

06A
RENONQUET
REEF

04A
ORTAC

06A
LES CASQUETS ROCK

SARK, BRECQHOU, HERM, JETHOU AND OFFSHORE ISLETS

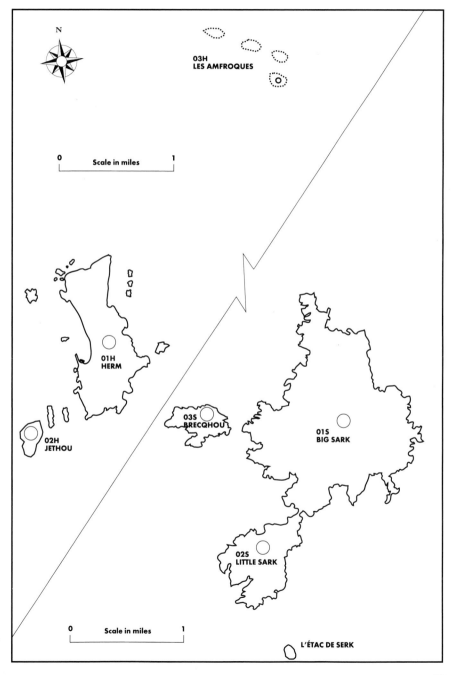

SITE ACCOUNTS: JERSEY

Jersey - Important Bird Areas
which meet the criteria for IBA status

Heathlands (Jersey Heathland IBA) composed of:

Heathlands (north coast)

Heathlands (south west coast)

Jersey Shoreline IBA

Heathland sites

Lowland heathland is an important habitat supporting a unique assemblage of plants and animals. Its importance is recognised by special reference in a European Directive. The coastal heaths combine to form an Important Bird Area.

HEATHLANDS (NORTH COAST)

01J   LES LANDES, ST OUEN
OS Sheet: Jersey. Grid Ref: WV550555.   **Area: 99ha.**

A coastal headland dominating the north-west corner of Jersey, consisting of large areas of bell heather and gorse. The area was designated as a Site of Scientific Interest (SSI) in 1996.

Site description
Les Landes is the largest and most important area of heathland in Jersey. The main gorse area is located to the south end and contains the largest concentration of Dartford warblers to be found in the island. The heather areas are mostly to be found on the western fringe, above the west facing cliffs. In the centre and north is a racecourse with rough grass and bracken within the actual racing circle. This area often provides a winter roost for short-eared owls and hen harriers. Some German-built emplacements, and an ancient castle on the north-west edge provide an area of interest for visitors. The site is bounded by steep coastal cliffs to the south, west and north, and by cultivated fields to the east.

Birds
Breeding **Dartford warblers** (5-10 pairs), **stonechats** (1-5 pairs), **wheatears** (1-3 pairs)**, skylarks** (5-10 pairs), **linnets** (10-30 pairs) and **raven** (1 pair). **Peregrines** are regular and may have attempted to breed in 1996. **Sparrowhawks** breed nearby and regularly hunt over the heath. Winter visitors include **short-eared owl, hen harrier** and **merlin**. Many migrants pass through the area and species such as **yellow wagtail, whinchat, snow bunting, lapland bunting, black redstart** and **dotterel** are regular, with **Richard's pipit** being recorded in most years recently.

Conservation issues
The area is under great pressure through recreational pursuits. Apart from the racecourse, where a new grandstand has been approved, a model aircraft flying site is located in the centre. Dog walking is popular and the site is regularly suggested as the location for another golf course. Gorse fires occur annually and are usually large with the southern end of the heathland being badly affected in 1996.

02J   CRABBÉ (Rouge Nez), ST MARY
OS Sheet: Jersey. Grid Ref: WV588555.   **Area: 12ha.**

A coastal headland on the north coast dominated by gorse and containing breeding **Dartford warbler**, **stonechat** and **yellowhammer**.

Site description
A small coastal headland dominated by gorse with localised bracken invasion. The site is used by the States of Jersey Defence Committee for the storage of explosives which prevents access by the general public.

Birds
Breeding **Dartford warblers**, **stonechats**, **skylarks** and **linnets**. **Yellowhammers** also breed. The site and those in the immediate vicinity, particularly the shooting range, are important wintering areas for all these species. Actual breeding numbers are unavailable due to the restricted access to the site.

Conservation issues
In need of management, the area suffers from excessive rabbit grazing and disturbance from a nearby shooting range. A proposal to site a go-kart race track on, or adjacent to, the area offers a threat to the site's future.

03J   LA TÊTE DE FRÉMONT (Frémont Point to Wolf's Caves), ST JOHN
OS Sheet: Jersey. Grid Ref: WV641562.   **Area: 12ha.**

A small area of heath along the north coast, dominated by gorse on a steep coastal slope.

Site description
Located in the centre of the north coast, this fragmented site provides the necessary habitat requirements for gorse-nesting species such as Dartford warbler. The area extends from Wolf's Caves in the west to the headland immediately west of Bonne Nuit Bay. The narrow strip of gorse expands into a more substantial area of gorse at La Tête de Frémont. The entire area is bordered by steep cliffs to the north and agricultural fields to the south.

Birds
Breeding **Dartford warbler** (1-2 pairs), **stonechat** (1-2 pairs), **yellowhammer** (1 pair), **linnet** (10+ pairs), **whitethroat** (1-2 pairs) and occasional **lesser whitethroat**. **Lesser black-backed gulls** breed on the cliffs to the north.

Conservation issues
Suffers from disturbance caused by the nearby cliffpath and bracken invasion of the gorse. Requires management. A large furze fire severely damaged around 70% of the area in 1996.

04J   LES PLATONS / EGYPT, TRINITY
OS Sheet: Jersey. Grid Ref: WV653556.   **Area: 24ha.**

A common dominated by bell heather with scattered gorse and conifer trees. It is a proposed SSI.

Site description
A north coast site containing fairly extensive but scattered areas of gorse and heather. Some cliff areas suffer from bracken invasion. The skyline of Les Platons is dominated by a radio transmitter mast and radar equipment. Scattered gorse extends north from Les Platons to La Belle Hougue Point. Bordered by cliffs on three sides and cultivated fields to the south.

Birds
Breeding **Dartford warbler** (3 pairs in 1996) at La Belle Hougue with further individual birds at Egypt and Les Platons. **Yellowhammer** breed at several points along the coastal strips (2-4 pairs). **Linnet** commonly breed and occasional breeding has been recorded of **whitethroat** and **lesser whitethroat** (1 pair in 1993).

Conservation issues
Suffers in certain areas from considerable bracken invasion and from disturbance from the nearby cliffpath. The gorse at Egypt is degenerate and in need of active management.

05J   LES HURETS, TRINITY
OS Sheet: Jersey. Grid Ref: WV668548.   **Area: 12ha.**

A dense stand of gorse on a steep slope stretching from La Chrétienne towards the west of Bouley Bay.

Site description
Another of the north coast's isolated chains of heathland dominated by bell heather and scattered gorse. The site was damaged by fire in the late 1980s and, due to bracken invasion, is in need of management. Bordered by cliffs to the east and north-east, steeply sloping fields to the west, and Bouley Bay to the south.

Birds
Both **Dartford warbler** and **stonechat** held territories in the 1993 survey: two pairs of the former bred in 1996. **Linnet** breed (1-5 pairs) and **herring gull** and **lesser black-backed gull** nest on the nearby cliffs.

Conservation issues
50% of the site was damaged by fire in 1995 and a further 20% in 1996. The remaining area is in need of management.

06J LE JARDIN D'OLIVET, TRINITY
OS Sheet: Jersey. Grid Ref: WV673542.   **Area: 25ha.**

A coastal heath above the granite cliffs of the island's north coast. The site is a proposed SSI.

Site description
The area is dominated by bell heather and scattered gorse. Wall lizards were present during 1992. Bordered by Bouley Bay in the north, a small valley and stream to the east, and large private gardens and cultivated fields to the south.

Birds
Breeding **Dartford warbler** (1-2 pairs), **stonechat** (1 pair), **whitethroat** (1-2 pairs) and **yellowhammer** (1 pair in 1993).

Conservation issues
Much of the gorse is degenerate and the area suffers from localised bracken invasion and excessive recreational use. Requires active management.

HEATHLANDS (SOUTH-WEST COAST)

07J NOIRMONT, ST BRELADE
OS Sheet: Jersey. Grid Ref: WV607471.   **Area: 39ha.**

A coastal headland on the south-west coast with scattered gorse, a few cultivated fields and a small area of woodland to the north-east. The area is a proposed SSI.

Site description
An exposed coastal headland with fragmented areas of scattered gorse and heather. Some parts are fenced off and under cultivation. Towards the southern cliff edge there is a small pond while a mixed woodland and small conifer plantation exists along the northern boundary. Noirmont is bordered by steep cliffs to the west, south and east.

Birds
The headland is a site for some of Jersey's most significant spring and autumn migration landfalls. Breeding species include **Dartford warbler** (1-2 pairs), **stonechat** (2-3 pairs), **whitethroat** (2-5 pairs), **linnet** (20 pairs) and **great spotted woodpecker** (1 pair). Depending upon the amount of agricultural activity, **skylarks** also breed. **Barn owls** and **sparrowhawks** nest nearby and hunt in the area.

Conservation issues
Due to its popularity the site suffers from considerable recreational disturbance at all times of the year. There are also problems from bracken invasion, agricultural land claims and inappropriate management of the gorse areas. The wooded areas were severely

damaged in the great storm of October 1987, and much sympathetic tree planting has taken place since.

08J   PORTELET COMMON, ST BRELADE
OS Sheet: Jersey. Grid Ref: WV596474.   **Area: 27ha.**

A cliff-top area of gorse and heather heathland on the island's south-west coast. The site is a proposed SSI.

Site description
An area of common dominated by gorse and situated above the island's south-west facing cliffs. Extensive bell heather lies to the south and a belt of holm oak extends to the east. Portelet is connected to Le Ouaisné and Noirmont by a gorse and conifer plantation providing an escape corridor in the event of fire. The site is bordered by a ridge leading down to Le Ouaisné Common in the north-west, by cliffs to the south-west, and by hotels and private houses to the east.

Birds
Breeding birds include **Dartford warblers** (3 pairs in 1996), **stonechat** (1-2 pairs), **whitethroat** (1-3 pairs) and **linnet** (10 pairs). **Cuckoo** also breed in most years. It is an important site for **cirl bunting** (1-3 pairs) given that these birds normally prefer to nest in 'clusters' on Le Ouaisné Common. **Swifts** breed in the cliffs to the west and a **gull** colony (**herring, lesser black-backed** and, a few **great black-backed**), is present at the southern end.

Conservation issues
In the past, the site has been damaged by vehicular access although this problem has now been addressed. A programme of conservation management is currently being undertaken to recover certain areas of gorse and to control the invasion of bracken.

09J   LE OUAISNÉ COMMON, ST BRELADE
OS Sheet: Jersey. Grid Ref: WV596479.   **Area: 10ha.**

An area of stabilised dry heath, sand dune slack and gorse, isolated from the seashore by a defensive seawall. This site is a proposed SSI with designation likely to be approved by the States during 1997.

Site description
Le Ouaisné is dominated by managed gorse and has a pond and reedbed fringed with willows on its eastern edge. To the north-west is an area of privately managed land with a large open field which is retained as fallow land. This land formerly had a boundary of extensive pine trees, many of which were lost in the great storm of October 1987. The site is low-lying and is bordered by ridges to the west, north and east, and by a seawall to the south.

Birds
Breeding **Dartford warbler** (2-3 pairs), **stonechat** (1-2 pairs), **serin** (1-3 pairs) and **whitethroat** (1-2 pairs). During most years **cuckoos** breed in the area. **Cirl bunting** breed on the ridge to the west, north and east (2-4 pairs), with the privately owned field to the north-west being an important winter feeding ground for them. The site also supports the agile frog, grass snake and green lizard.

Conservation issues
The area suffers from increasing recreational pressures, building development and drainage in the periphery. Fly tipping and invasive bracken are other localised problems. In recent years however, a programme of gorse management has greatly improved the area. Furze fires in 1995 and 1996 damaged small but significant areas of the gorse.

10J   LA LANDE DU OUEST (Gorselands, La Moye), ST BRELADE
OS Sheet: Jersey. Grid Ref: WV565475.   **Area: 20ha.**

Purchased by the States of Jersey in 1993. A cliff-top area of gorse heathland in the south-west of the Island. This site was designated an SSI in 1996.

Site description
This site, known as Gorselands, is predominantly gorse heathland. Although the coastal edge was damaged by fire in 1989, it is now dominated by Yorkshire fog, bracken and, in certain areas on the cliff edge, by Hottentot fig. Bordered by cliffs to the south, a housing estate to the north, La Moye Prison to the east, and the island's desalination plant to the west.

Birds

Breeding **Dartford warbler** (3 pairs in 1996), **stonechat** (1-2 pairs), **whitethroat** (2-4 pairs), **cirl bunting** (1 pair), **skylark** (2 pairs), **serin** (1-2 pairs) and **linnet** (5-10 pairs). A pair of **ravens** bred in 1994 and **barn owl**, which hunt over the heathland, also breed in the vicinity of the desalination plant.

Conservation issues

The area has been, and still is, under threat from several activities including excessive recreational usage and vehicular access on the south side (now banned). The north end of the site is also sometimes used as a car park by residents of the nearby housing estate. A fire during 1989 badly affected a large area of gorse which has still not regenerated. There is a continuous localised problem of Hottentot fig on the cliff-tops.

11J   LE BEAUPORT / LES CREUX, ST BRELADE
OS Sheet: Jersey. Grid Ref: WV580479.   **Area: 10ha.**

A common dominated by gorse above the granite cliffs. The thin belt of heathland stretches along the coast westwards above Les Ieaux de Ficquet and eastwards to Les Creux (above St. Brelade's Bay).

Site description

A narrow strip of heathland which stretches from Les Creux in the east to Les Ieaux de Ficquet in the west. The site is bordered by steep cliffs to the south, cultivated fields to the north, and a housing estate to the west. A decision by the States of Jersey to designate an area to the north of the gorse as a future golf course was rescinded in 1994, although proposals for a natural area providing for informal recreation are being considered. The future use of the land is at present uncertain. While one area suffers from excessive recreational erosion, another is affected by the dumping of agricultural waste.

Birds

Breeding **cirl bunting** (1 pair), **stonechat** (1 pair), **whitethroat** (2-5 pairs) and **linnet** (5-10 pairs). **Dartford warblers**, which once nested on a regular basis, now breed only occasionally. **Ravens** breed on the cliffs at Fliquet (1 pair) and **swifts** and **kestrels** (1 pair) regularly nest in the cliffs at the southern boundary. A pair of **sparrowhawks** bred in 1995 and 1996.

Conservation issues

Much of the gorse is degenerate, and a large furze fire destroyed most of the gorse heathland at Beauport in 1996. The area at Les Creux which was similarly damaged in 1990, has only partially recovered.

12J   L'ÉTACQ, ST OUEN
OS Sheet: Jersey. Grid Ref: WV560543 to WV552549.   **Area: 18ha.**

Coastal cliffs dominated by gorse separating Le Bas de L'Étacq from La Girouette.

Site description
A common scattered with bell heather to the north, with dense gorse extending down the cliffs on the western and southern sides. Bordered by cliffs to the south and west and cultivated land to the north. Two roads divide the area from the extensive gorse heathland of Les Landes. There is a quarry to the south.

Birds
Breeding **Dartford warbler** (2-7 pairs), **stonechat** (1 pair) and **linnet** (2-5 pairs).

Conservation issues
This series of small gorse headlands, coupled with the gorse area at the south end of Les Landes represents the most important area remaining in Jersey for breeding Dartford warbler (at least 7 singing males in 1995). The gorse in some areas is in need of management. Separate furze fires in 1995 and 1996 have severely damaged the majority of the known Dartford warbler breeding sites.

13J   LE MONT ROSSIGNOL, ST OUEN/ST PETER
OS Sheet: Jersey. Grid Ref: WV575520.   **Area: 15ha.**

Scattered gorse on steep foothills overlooking St. Ouen's coastal plain in the west of the island.

Site description
A series of discontinuous gorse headlands to the east of St. Ouen's coastal plain, the main gorse areas occurring at Le Mont Rossignol and La Grande Cueillette, with the remaining areas bracken covered. Bordered by the coastal plain to the west, a valley leading to Val de la Mare reservoir to the south, cultivated fields to the east and Le Mont Matthieu to the north.

Birds
Breeding **Dartford warbler** (1-3 pairs), **stonechat** (1-2 pairs), **whitethroat** (1-3 pairs) and **lesser whitethroat** (1-2 pairs).

Conservation issues
Much of the gorse on these headlands is degenerate, and there is considerable bracken invasion in some areas.

14J   LE MONT À LA BRUNE / LE MONT DU JUBILÉ, ST PETER
OS Sheet: Jersey. Grid Ref: WV578507 and WV583513.   **Area: 20ha.**

Scattered gorse on steep slopes to the west of the airport.

Site description
An area of scattered gorse on the ridge east of St. Ouen's Bay coastal plain. Bordered by the airport to the east, Le Mont à la Brune public road to the south and the valley of Val de la Mare reservoir to the north.

Birds
Breeding **linnet** (2-5 pairs). Formerly held breeding **Dartford warbler**, which now nests only occasionally due to the condition of the gorse. **Barn owl** regularly breed at Val de la Mare.

Conservation issues
Much of the gorse is degenerate and the whole area suffers from a lack of management. There is much bracken invasion and agricultural usage on the lower slopes.

15J   PETIT PORT, ST BRELADE
OS Sheet: Jersey. Grid Ref: WV560487.   **Area: 6ha.**

A small headland dividing Petit Port Bay from St Ouen's Bay in the south-west of the island.

Site description
A small, steeply sloping headland, with gorse on the south facing slope and to a lesser extent, on the top. The gorse extends back into a narrow valley where it is mostly degenerate. The valley has a small stream and is thickly wooded with willow; these willows being attractive to migrant birds, especially warblers. The north slope of the headland is mostly bracken covered. Bounded by Petit Port Bay to the south, St Ouen's Bay to the north, cliffs to the west and housing development to the east.

Birds
Breeding **Dartford warbler** (1 pair), **stonechat** (1 pair) and **linnet** (1-10 pairs). **Marsh warbler** formerly bred in the small valley. Many migrant species are recorded each year including in recent years such scarce birds as **red-backed shrike**, **wryneck**, **nightjar**, **black redstart** and **melodious warbler**. Both **grey heron** and **little egret** use trees in the valley as an occasional roost site.

Conservation issues
The gorse is in need of management and fires are an annual threat to the area, which is a popular recreational spot. Some of the main gorse area on the south slope has recently been grubbed out for potato growing, as has the valley area above where marsh warblers formerly bred.

Jersey Shoreline IBA

16J   JERSEY SHORELINE
OS Sheet: Jersey. Grid Ref: WV546552 in west to WV715530 in east.

Area: 3100ha. (approx.)

The area covers the whole intertidal zone from L'Étacq in the north-west, via the south coast to La Rocque in the south-east, then north through Grouville Bay to St. Catherine's in the north-east. Several locations are likely SSIs. The south-east coastline between La Collette and La Rocque, including Grouville Bay, is likely to be designated in 1997; at which time Ramsar designation will be sought. This part of Jersey's coastline meets the criteria for designation under the Ramsar Convention.

Site description
Extensive intertidal zones exist providing large areas for both waders and geese to feed, especially at low tide. Considerable areas of sand and silt occur in St. Ouen's Bay to the west, St. Aubin's Bay to the south and Grouville Bay in the east. Important winter wader roosts occur at several locations, notably L'Étacq and Le Petit Port on the west coast, St. Aubin's Fort, Elizabeth Castle, La Collette, Green Island, Le Hocq, Pontac and La Rocque on the south and south-east coasts. The rock on which Icho Tower stands isolated off the south-east coast also has a significant high tide wader roost.

Birds
Brent geese winter in UK nationally important numbers with up to 1200, increasing to 1700 in hard winters; these numbers including up to 100 **light-bellied brent geese** (*B. b. hrota*) originating from the Canadian arctic. **Little egrets** increasingly winter here, with up to 150 present in late 1996. At least 8000 waders winter on these shorelines each year and those whose numbers are of UK national importance, or closely approaching it are: **sanderling** (449), **grey plover** (722), **turnstone** (693), **ringed plover** (490). These figures were the maxima recorded during winter counts 1991-1996. Breeding waders include **oystercatchers** (5-10 pairs) and **ringed plovers** (1-5 pairs).

Conservation issues
The shoreline is threatened by coastal pollution, potential marina developments, and land reclamation schemes, especially in the area of La Collette, West Park, St Aubin and Gorey Harbour. The States of Jersey agreed, in principle, in 1996 to reclamation at St Aubin, which is one of the two main feeding sites of light-bellied brent geese. Shellfish farming in the south-east of the area may also develop into a conservation issue.

Jersey - Sites of Channel Islands Importance for Birds
which do not meet the criteria for IBA status

Seabird Colonies

While not of IBA status the seabird colonies of Jersey are of great significance holding important breeding populations of birds such as terns.

17J   LES ÉCRÉHOUS, ST MARTIN
Lat: 49°17'N Long: 01°56'W   Area: 0.2 to 40.7 km² (approx.) (dependent upon state of tide)

A reef located 10km off the north-east coast of Jersey. The 1996 Annual Report to the States of Jersey by the Environmental Adviser says of Les Écréhous and Plateau des Minquiers; "...... Les Minquiers and Les Écréhous, are of considerable marine ecological importance as has become evident from initial survey work at the former location. These sites may very well warrant SSI designation in the fullness of time but there does seem a case for the urgent "special" designation to conserve not only the ecological value of these reefs but also their unique character."

Site description
A group of small islets and rocks to the north-east of Jersey which are for the most part devoid of vegetation. The most southerly and largest of the islands is La Maître Île, which has an extensive area of tree mallow covering its centre. The more northerly, La Marmotière, is mostly covered with small huts and other dwellings, but has a shingle bank extending to the north, which is sometimes breached by the spring tides. The area around this bank contains Jersey's largest breeding colony of common terns.

Birds
Breeding **common tern** (50-60 pairs 1995/6), **cormorant** (50-80 pairs), **oystercatcher** (5-10 pairs), **shag** (100+ pairs), **lesser black-backed gull** (0-5 pairs), **great black-backed gull** (12-15 pairs) and **herring gull** (380 pairs in 1996). The mallow on La Maître Île is an important refuge for migrant passerines.

Conservation issues
The common tern colony is subject to much human disturbance, and consequently breeding success is affected. The area of tree mallow on La Maître Île is also subjected to periodic human damage and clearance, reducing the amount of cover available for breeding seabirds and migrant passerines.

18J   ELIZABETH CASTLE, ST HELIER
OS Sheet: Jersey. Grid Ref: WV639476.   **Area: 5ha.**

Man-made tidal fortress and breakwater in St. Aubin's Bay.

Site description
The fortress in St Aubin's Bay is isolated from Jersey during the periods of high tide each day, and is otherwise connected by a causeway across the beach. There is little vegetation apart from a few fig trees outside the walls on the eastern side and several areas of lawn within the castle walls.

Birds
Breeding **common tern** (1-15 pairs: with 4 pairs in 1996), **oystercatcher** (2-4 pairs), occasional **black redstart** (1 pair) and **common swift** (50 pairs); 1 pair of **ringed plover** bred in 1995. The lawn within the castle walls has a regular flock of **brent geese** feeding in winter months (50-80 birds).

Conservation issues
The common tern colony which exists there is subject to disturbance from visitors to the castle and the firing of a cannon at noon during summer months. The breeding success rate is usually low. The area is threatened by increasing land reclamation schemes to the east and north-east.

19J   LE HOCQ, ST CLEMENT
OS Sheet: Jersey. Grid Ref: WV686465.   **Area: 1ha.**

One small rock to the south of Le Hocq point, containing the largest mainland colony of breeding common terns. It would be included in any SSI designation of this coastline.

Site description
A small rock, just south of the beach at Le Hocq, connected to the mainland at low tide and bordered by beach to the north and sea on the other sides.

Birds
Breeding **common tern** (19 pairs 1996) and **oystercatcher** (1 pair 1996). The rocks here also act as an important high tide roost for waders during winter months.

Conservation issues
The site suffers serious disturbance from visitors, both accidentally and sometimes deliberately. In recent years the colony of common terns has deserted as a result of disturbance.

20J   L'ÉTACQUEREL FORT / BOULEY BAY, TRINITY
OS Sheet: Jersey. Grid Ref: WV680546.   **Area: 1ha.**

A small fort, built into the cliff-side to the east of Bouley Bay.

Site description
This small fort, on Jersey's north coast, to the east of Bouley Bay, contains a colony of breeding common terns. This site is also important for wall lizard.

Birds
Breeding **common tern** (8 pairs 1992) both here and on adjacent rocks, **oystercatcher** (1 pair) and **great black-backed gull** (1 pair).

Conservation issues
The cliff site is accessible from all sides and is therefore subject to much disturbance and the common terns often desert during breeding. Predation by brown rats is also a problem.

21J   NORTH COAST CLIFFS
OS Sheet: Jersey. Grid Ref: WV547549 to WV710540.   **Area: 2500ha. (approx.)**

Mostly sheer cliffs rising to over 100 metres above sea level in many places, occasionally interrupted by small north facing valleys.

Site description
The cliffs cover the whole north coast of Jersey from L'Étacq in the west to St Catherine's in the east, and are interrupted by small valleys at several points and by seven small sheltered bays with either sandy or stony beaches. Along most of their length the cliffs are bordered to the south by cultivated fields. The whole cliff area provides important breeding sites for seabirds. Of particular importance are:

PLÉMONT WV566566. Breeding site for **puffin**, **razorbill** and **fulmar**.

LE GRAND BECQUET WV575562. Breeding **puffin**, **razorbill** and **fulmar**.

Birds
Breeding **puffin** (10-20 pairs), **razorbill** (1-5 pairs), **fulmar** (100+ pairs), **common tern** (0-10 pairs), **lesser black-backed gull** (50+ pairs, increasing), **shag** (300 pairs), **herring gull** (500+ pairs) **great black-backed gull** (20+ pairs), **raven** (3-5 pairs). **Peregrine falcon** formerly bred and may do so again. **Yellowhammers** breed on the clifftops (30+ pairs), their main Jersey stronghold, as do **stonechats** (10+ pairs) and occasional **whitethroat** and **lesser whitethroat**.

Conservation issues

The cliffs have paths established along almost all of their length. These paths are attracting not only walkers but also mountain bikers and in some places horse riders. Some of the main colonies suffer periodic human disturbance, both accidental and sometimes deliberate. Rubbish dumping is a problem in a few areas.

22J   LE PLATEAU DES MINQUIERS, GROUVILLE
Lat: 48°58'N   Long: 02°04'W   Area: 0.1 to 115km² (approx.) (dependent upon state of the tide)

An extensive area of rocks and sand, located 20km south of Jersey. See the comments under Site 17J above.

Site description

The area consists of a large area of rock and sand, exposed at low tide. The only significant area of vegetation, tree mallow, is found on the main islet, La Maîtresse Île and provides important cover and feeding opportunities for migrant passerines. At low tide an area in excess of 100 sq km is exposed, this decreasing to little more than 0.1 ha at the highest tide. La Maîtresse Île is largely covered by man-made structures, mostly small stone huts.

Birds

Breeding **shag** (50 pairs in 1996) and **cormorant** (20+ pairs in 1996). The extensive intertidal area provides feeding for large numbers of waders during passage periods and in winter, and the tree mallow on La Maîtresse Île is an important refuge for passage migrants.

Conservation issues

There is much human disturbance from time to time on La Maîtresse Île and a helicopter landing pad is located on the east end of the islet, though infrequently used.

23J   SOUTH-WEST CLIFFS, ST BRELADE
OS Sheet: Jersey. Grid Ref: WV610475 to WV550481.   Area: 800ha. (approx.)

An area of mostly steep or sheer cliffs extending from Noirmont in the east to La Corbière in the west.

Site description

Similar in appearance to the north coast cliffs, although generally not more than 60 metres above sea level, these cliffs provide important breeding sites for seabirds. Bordered by gorse heathland to the north along much of their length, with St. Brelade's Bay creating a break between the cliff area at Portelet and Beauport.

Birds

Breeding **shag** (50+ pairs), **herring gull** (200+ pairs), **lesser black-backed gull** (30+ pairs), **great black-backed gull** (10+ pairs) and **raven** (1-2 pairs). **Fulmars** have been prospecting the cliffs for several years and **cirl bunting** breed at several sites on the cliff top area.

Conservation issues

Some areas suffer from considerable bracken invasion and Hottentot fig is a serious problem at several sites, notably Noirmont, Beauport and La Moye.

Wetland Sites

24J   LA MARE AU SEIGNEUR (St Ouen's Pond), ST PETER/ST OUEN

OS Sheet: Jersey. Grid Ref: WV567520.   **Area: 10ha. (approx.)**

St. Ouen's Pond is five hectares of open freshwater, surrounded by an extensive bed of common reed. It is a proposed SSI.

Site description

St. Ouen's Pond is the largest area of natural freshwater in the Channel Islands. The pond receives the majority of its water from a stream flowing from the south. There is a small canal to the north of the reedbed and the remnant of another to the south. A wet area on the southern fringe of the reedbed provides important habitat for ducks and waders. Bordered by Les Mielles to the north, cultivated fields to the east, a golf course to the south and a main road and seawall to the west.

Birds

Breeding **Cetti's warbler** (10-20 pairs), **reed warbler** (50-100 pairs), **sedge warbler** (0-5 pairs), **lapwing** (10-20 pairs), **stonechat** (0-3 pairs), **shoveler** (1-3 pairs), **little grebe** (1-2 pairs), **pochard** (3 pairs 1993), **skylark** (10-20 pairs), **bearded tit** (1-2 pairs). The area is very important for passage migrants, and offers wintering areas for such birds as **hen harrier, short-eared owl, peregrine falcon, bittern** (1-3 birds 1994 and 1995), and ducks: including **wigeon, teal, gadwall** and **shoveler**. A pair of **marsh harrier** attempted to breed in 1996.

An actively worked sand-pit at le Mont à la Brune contain's Jersey's only significant colony of **sand martins** (50-100 pairs), and these birds regularly feed over St Ouen's Pond.

Conservation issues

The site is under increasing pressure from water extraction and recreational use, including a recently created golf course to the south.

25J   GROUVILLE MARSH, GROUVILLE
OS Sheet: Jersey. Grid Ref: WV698493.   **Area: 11ha.**

A complex low-lying wetland close to the east coast of the island. It is a proposed SSI.

Site description
The site consists of wet meadows at the eastern end, dense willow scrub in the centre and reedbeds at the western end. An area of shallow ponds has recently been created to the northern end. Bordered by a public road and housing to the east, cultivated fields to the south and west and a housing development to the north.

Birds
Breeding **Cetti's warbler** (1 pair), **great spotted woodpecker** (1 pair), **lesser spotted woodpecker** (0-1 pair), **reed warbler** (10-30 pairs). A very important refuge for passage migrants and winter visitors. **Long-eared owls** use the marsh as a roost site and **barn owls** hunt over the area. **Cirl bunting** feed in the rough grass areas during the winter.

Conservation issues
The area is threatened by drainage, housing development, agricultural land claim and excessive management on the periphery.

26J   LONGUEVILLE MARSH (Les Prés Dormant), St SAVIOUR
OS Sheet: Jersey. Grid Ref: WV675480.   **Area: 10ha.**

A small, low-lying wetland marsh in the south-east of the island. It is a proposed SSI.

Site description
The site consists of a reedbed surrounded by improved grazing meadows. Bordered by a trading estate and housing to the west, cultivated fields to the east and south and a public road and housing to the north. The island's largest heron and egret roost exists on the eastern boundary.

Birds
Breeding **reed warbler** (5-10 pairs), **Cetti's warbler** (0-1 pair), **skylark** (1-5 pairs) and occasional **lapwing**. Up to 120 **grey herons** and 150 **little egrets** (1996) use the trees on the eastern boundary as a roost. It is also an important refuge for passage migrants and winter visitors.

Conservation issues
It has been much degraded in recent years and continues to be threatened by industrial expansion and housing development, by agricultural intensification and by a lack of conservation management.

Grassland

27J PONT MARQUET, ST BRELADE
OS Sheet: Jersey. Grid Ref: WV588495. **Area: 5ha.**

A small semi-managed area of rough grass, scrub and woodland in the west of the island.

Site description
Officially described as a Country Park, the area consists of a rough grass field, bordered by public roads to the south, south-east and west, a housing development and fields, some cultivated, to the north. Within these boundaries are small areas of scrub, mixed woodland and several large pine trees as well as two small man-made ponds. To the immediate north is an unimproved grass field containing an area of largely degenerate gorse.

Birds
The area's main importance comes from the presence of 1-3 pairs of **cirl bunting** breeding in the area itself, as well as in the unimproved fields to the north. **Serin** (5-10 pairs) breed in their most concentrated numbers in Jersey. Other breeding birds include **barn owl** (1 pair), **great spotted woodpecker** (1 pair) and occasional **coal tit**. **Grey wagtail** and **kingfisher** often winter.

Conservation issues
The area is threatened by recreational disturbance, notably dog-walking, some agricultural land claim, and especially over-management which threatens the viability of the cirl bunting population.

28J LES QUENNEVAIS / LA MOYE, ST BRELADE
OS Sheet: Jersey. Grid Ref: WV575496. **Area: 45ha.**

An area of sand dune and heathland on top of the west-facing ridge at the south-west of the island; now occupied by La Moye Golf Course. The dunes were designated as an SSI in 1996.

Site description
An area formerly dominated by gorse both in the centre and around the fringes, as well as some short and long rough grass which, together with stands of mostly isolated coniferous trees, provides the best habitat remaining in Jersey for cirl buntings. Bounded by a ridge with sand dunes to the west, a valley containing scrub and blackthorn to the north, playing fields to the east and a housing development to the south.

Birds
This site, together with Grouville golf course on the east coast, contains the majority of breeding **cirl buntings** remaining in Jersey (4-6 pairs). There are also breeding **serin** (1-5 pairs) and **linnet** (5-20 pairs).

Conservation issues

The habitat requirements of cirl buntings here are precise, particularly with regard to feeding areas of long and short rough grass and the current management regime of the golf course provides these. Any change in management practice to a more manicured course would almost certainly result in the loss of this species from the area, and seriously threaten its continued presence on the island as a whole; given its preference for breeding in "clusters".

29J   GOREY COMMON, GROUVILLE
OS Sheet: Jersey. Grid Ref: WV700495.   **Area: 36ha.**

An area of gorse common, above the sea wall at Gorey, now occupied by the Royal Jersey Golf Course.

Site description

The whole site is occupied by a managed golf course but still retains significant areas of gorse and both long and short rough grass with some areas of scrub and mature trees on the western fringe. Bounded by a main road and Grouville Marsh to the west, housing to the south and south-west, a sea wall to the east and a car park to the north.

Birds

As with the area of La Moye golf course in the south-west of the island, the present management regime of the site provides the best remaining habitat in the island for **cirl buntings** (3-5 pairs). The scrub area on the western side provides suitable habitat for occasional breeding **whitethroat**, **lesser whitethroat** as well as **linnet**. **Cetti's warblers** have been recorded on occasions, probably as a result of the close proximity of Grouville Marsh. Migrant birds recorded on a more or less regular basis include: **wheatear**, **whinchat**, **garden warbler**, **skylark** and both **snow bunting** and **lapland bunting**.

Conservation issues

Cirl buntings feed in both short and long rough grass on the edges of the golf course fairways, as well as on grass seeds left on the pathways from grass cutting. They breed within the remaining stands of gorse, despite considerable disturbance from golfers and also walkers who frequent the common area. The present management regime is sympathetic to the birds' requirements but any change to a more manicured golf course could rapidly result in the loss of cirl buntings from this, the only regular breeding site in the east of the island and thus threaten the viability of the species within Jersey.

Wooded Inland Valleys

30J WOODED INLAND VALLEYS
OS Sheet: Jersey - Refs: (see below).   **Area (see below).**

A series of narrow valleys, mostly orientated north to south which provide the main bulk of suitable habitat for Jersey's woodland species.

Site description
For the most part these valleys consist of a narrow band of mixed woodland rising steeply on either side, often with cultivated fields on the high ground above. Most have a public road running through the centre of the valley along their entire length, and some also contain bodies of water, mostly in the form of artificially created reservoirs. In addition to being the most important sites for breeding woodland species, they also provide refuge and feeding for passage migrants and winter visitors in times of stress through extreme weather. Some of the more important valleys are:

ST PETER'S VALLEY, ST PETER. WV617505 to WV602532. Area: 175ha.
A proposed SSI. Includes a small reservoir at La Hague. An important area for **lesser spotted woodpecker**. **Sparrowhawk** bred in 1996, and **long-eared owl** may also have done so.

WATERWORKS VALLEY, ST HELIER/ST LAWRENCE. WV631502 to WV634541. Area 200ha.
Includes the reservoirs of Handois, Dannemarche and Millbrook. A pair of **kingfishers** bred here in 1989, and have probably done so since. This is also a breeding site for **lesser spotted woodpecker**.

LES VAUX DE LECQ, ST OUEN/ST MARY. WV593547 to WV583553. Area: 50ha.
A proposed SSI. A narrow valley, well wooded to the west, with agricultural fields on the eastern slope.

ST. LAWRENCE VALLEY, ST LAWRENCE. WV617508 to WV624520. Area: 60ha.
A secluded valley with little public access and no public road. **Lesser spotted** and **great spotted woodpeckers** are regular.

FERN VALLEY, ST HELIER/ST LAWRENCE. WV655498 to WV641524. Area: 50ha.
Another secluded valley with little public access, although a short footpath walk has recently been created.

LA VALLÉE DES VAUX, ST HELIER. WV655498 to WV652515. Area: 40ha.
Much of the lower part of this valley is occupied by housing of a low density, with only narrow wooded areas existing on the valley sides.

LES GRANDS VAUX, ST HELIER/ST SAVIOUR/TRINITY. WV665507 to WV6685224. Area: 60ha.
High density housing occupies most of the lower valley and a large reservoir occupies the centre, with a small pond above. To the north of this reservoir is an area closed to the public and it is this area which provides most of the ornithological interest. **Siskins** are regular outside the breeding season, mainly on alders, and **sparrowhawks** probably bred in 1994. **Lesser spotted woodpeckers** are recorded occasionally.

SWISS VALLEY, ST SAVIOUR. WV673486 to WV673498. Area: 25ha.
A small, secluded valley with little public access in the east of the island.

ST. CATHERINE'S WOOD, ST MARTIN. WV705525 to WV697534. Area: 30ha.
A proposed SSI. An important valley close to the coast on the north-east of the island. A small reservoir exists at the southern end. The woodland is some of the most mature to be found in Jersey and is a regular location for **sparrowhawk, lesser spotted woodpecker**, **great spotted woodpecker** and breeding **spotted flycatcher**. **Wood warbler** and occasionally **golden oriole** are recorded on passage.

ROZEL WOODS, ST MARTIN/TRINITY. WV696544 to WV683544. Area: 30ha.
Most of the woodland in this valley is privately owned and not open to the public.

MOURIER VALLEY, ST MARY. WV615554 to WV608562. Area: 20ha.
A small valley running down to the sea through a gap in the north coast cliffs. Scrub and bracken, with some gorse at the northern end give way to a small reservoir in the centre and mixed woodland above. A small track runs down the centre of the valley, but no public road. It provides an important area for arriving migrants to find refuge and feed. **Yellowhammer** breed (1-2 pairs).

LE MONT LES VAUX, ST BRELADE. WV602489 to WV593495. Area: 26ha.
The Railway Walk follows this valley from St. Aubin's to Red Houses. Although narrow, it provides important habitat for both migrants and winter visitors. **Grey herons** are regular at a small reservoir half way up the valley and **lesser spotted woodpeckers** have bred.

LE VAL DE LA MARE, ST PETER/ST OUEN. WV578519 to WV589526. Area: 50ha.
A west facing valley, inland from the coastal plain in which St. Ouen's Pond is located. At the western end of the valley is a large reservoir, which through the nature of its construction attracts little bird life. Occasionally **little grebes** breed. At the top of one branch of the reservoir is a very small reedbed, where **Cetti's warbler** (1 pair) and **reed warbler** (2-4 pairs) breed. The wooded areas above the reservoir provide diverse habitat for breeding birds and **sparrowhawk** bred in 1996. **Lesser whitethroat** bred in 1993.

QUEEN'S VALLEY, GROUVILLE/ ST SAVIOUR. WV694495 to WV697503. Area: 10ha.

This recently flooded valley was formerly an important area for passage migrants and breeding **long-eared owl**. Now much degraded in its value to woodland species, but the reservoir may prove of value to waterfowl in the future. **Cormorant** are regular outside the breeding season, and a wintering flock of **greenshank** (1-15 birds) roosts if water levels are reduced.

Birds

All the breeding species associated with woodland in Jersey may be found in the inland valleys of the island. Breeding species of note include **long-eared owl** (1-2 pairs), **barn owl** (10+ pairs), **great spotted woodpecker** (50 pairs), **lesser spotted woodpecker** (5+ pairs) and **short-toed treecreeper** (common). Occasional breeding records exist for **kingfisher**, **little grebe**, **tufted duck** and **wood warbler**. **Sparrowhawk** are regular (30+ birds 1996) and are breeding again after a 30 year absence.

Conservation issues

Many of the valleys are subject to great recreational disturbance, noise and other pollution from road traffic, agricultural land claim and in some areas, destruction of hedging. Over management or inappropriate management is a serious problem in some valleys, for example La Vallée des Vaux and Les Vaux de Lecq. Removal of vegetation from the surrounds of reservoirs also causes a severe problem in some areas, for example Queen's Valley and Le Val de la Mare.

SITE ACCOUNTS:
GUERNSEY

Guernsey - Important Bird Areas
which meet the criteria for IBA status

Heathlands (Guernsey Heathland IBA) composed of:

Shoreline (Guernsey Shoreline IBA) including :

Heathlands

01G   PLEINMONT, TORTEVAL
OS Sheet: Guernsey.   Grid Ref: WV240757.   **Area: 100ha.**

A cliff-top headland forming the south-western corner of Guernsey.

Site description
The mixture of small fields and non-cultivated land makes this the largest open area on the south coast. This site also contains small areas of remnant heathland. These provide a refuge to many birds when not disturbed. There is very limited development influence on the area and it remains as the premier site in Guernsey for the study of bird migration. The use of the fields for the cultivation of potatoes and other crops provides a rich and diverse habitat which is used by many migrant birds for resting and feeding. There are large areas of scrubby vegetation consisting of hawthorn, blackthorn, gorse and bracken interspersed with the agricultural land. The northern side is an escarpment to the sea. This slope has a good cover of trees both deciduous and coniferous which often provide shelter from the prevailing south-westerly winds. The southern edge is typical cliff habitat with a low grass sward and several rocky outcrops. There is good vehicular access to the headland and adequate parking. In general there is unrestricted access for walkers.

Birds
Many of the passerine migrants passing through Guernsey occur in their highest numbers at Pleinmont. The location and habitat provides a suitable stop-over for these birds. They are able to feed and put on reserves of fat for their migrations. Over 150 species of birds have been recorded from the area and at certain times of the year very large numbers of birds pass through. These include several thousand **skylark**, **meadow pipit** and **chaffinch** in late autumn. In winter this site has had up to five **short-eared owls** which roost in traditional locations. The breeding birds include **long-eared owl**, **sparrowhawk** and occasionally **black redstart**. In addition **whitethroat** (5-7 pairs), **stonechat** (8-10 pairs) and **linnet** (25-30 pairs) are present in summer. At least one pair of **Dartford warblers** breed in most years.

Conservation issues
There is considerable pressure to allow recreational activity over large areas. A motor cycle scramble track has been established which is used extensively in autumn and winter. Several fields have been seeded to monoculture grass and this has reduced the diversity of habitat available. There is continuing development around the fringes of the area and a tendency to use the site for events which are not possible in the more developed parts of the island.

02G L'ANCRESSE (including FORT LE MARCHANT and FORT DOYLE), VALE
OS Sheet: Guernsey. Grid Ref: WV343834.   **Area: 125ha.**

A low lying area of heathland common with gorse. A golf course has been created over most of the western end of the area.

Site description

The most extensive area of lowland common in the island. The creation of an 18 hole golf course across the major part of the site has reduced the natural habitat to fragmentary pockets. The eastern side is more heavily developed but there is considerably more gorse remaining. Small sections of scrub and tamarisk provide alternative feeding sites for migrant birds. Bracken encroachment is evident in several areas.

Birds

The only site in the north of the island which has **Dartford warbler** present. At least five pairs of **stonechat** also breed in the dense sections of gorse. During spring and autumn migration the position of the site on the north coast often allows for the build up of migrant birds. This is the first landfall after an over sea flight of at least 70 miles for birds from the south coast of England. Many take advantage to recuperate and replenish reserves of fat before moving on or dispersing inland. **Redstart, wheatear, whinchat** and **yellow wagtail** are species which can occur in 'falls' over the whole area. The short grass of the fairways and practice area of the golf course attract pipits and wagtails. Waders which prefer the short turf eg **dotterel** and **buff-breasted sandpiper** have also been found here on several occasions. There are four or five wet and marshy areas amongst the heather and gorse. These are used as drinking sites by passerines and feeding sites by many species. A very wide variety of species has been recorded and it remains one of the least developed areas on Guernsey.

Conservation issues

There are considerable pressures on the area. The golf course is used extensively often from dawn till dusk. In winter the shooting of legal game species creates disturbance. There are calls for the extension of the golf course towards Fort Doyle which would reduce the original habitat even further. At least one of the marshy areas has been filled in recently ostensibly to improve it for agricultural purposes.

03G   SOUTH COAST CLIFFS
OS Sheet: Guernsey.   Grid Ref: WV237760 (in the west) to WV344748 (in the east)
Area: 256ha.

Cliff and heathland dominated by gorse.

Site description
An extensive single habitat type. It stretches from Pleinmont in the west to La Vallette, St Peter Port in the east. The dominant vegetation is gorse and bracken with areas of hawthorn and blackthorn scrub. There are also small pockets of mature deciduous and coniferous woodland.

Birds
The main breeding area for **Dartford warblers** (3+ pairs) is centred on the south coast cliffs. The recovery of the species from total elimination as a breeding bird in 1986 has been sporadic but there were at least three pairs present in 1994. The survey work by Hill (1991) gives specific data on all the seabirds breeding on the cliffs, which include **fulmar** (15 pairs), **shag** (100 pairs), **lesser black-backed gull** (35 pairs), **herring gull** (550 pairs) and **great black-backed gull** (20 pairs). The only breeding site for **raven** is on the cliffs and with one other pair on Herm their status is continually under threat. The preservation and management of the gorse may allow **yellowhammers** to breed once again and possibly establish **cirl buntings** as a resident species. All areas of the cliffs are used by passage migrants for feeding and shelter.

Conservation issues
The major threat to the cliff land area is continued and unrestricted recreational disturbance. This includes motor cycle scrambling and four wheel drive tracks as well as shooting. There is a lack of co-ordinated management for the whole area with many different landowners. Bracken invasion is evident in several areas.

04G   GUERNSEY SHORELINE
OS Sheet: Guernsey.   Grid Ref: WV 340792 (in the east) to WV244762 (in the west)
Area: 550ha.

A rocky shoreline which runs north from St Peter Port, round the north coast and down the west coast to Pleinmont, with numerous small bays of both sand and shingle. There are a number of off-lying reefs and islets which greatly increases the area of habitat available.

Site description
The largest single habitat type in the island. There are many individual areas which together encompass the west, north and east coasts. The habitat varies and provides different species with their own particular requirements. Bay-head beaches and rocky headlands form the largest element. In addition there are storm beaches and shallow tidal areas which provide additional habitat types. The bays and reef areas also are used by many marine species especially as a refuge during adverse weather conditions.

Birds
The area is of national importance for wintering **ringed plover** (330) and of international importance for **turnstone** (730). Many other wading birds including **dunlin** and **oystercatchers** are present during winter. During migration up to 25 species of wader can be found. The principal feeding areas are centred on Richmond, Rocquaine, Belle Greve and Grande Havre. A number of roosting sites have been identified, eg Pecqueries, Miellette and Portinfer, and these are as important as the feeding grounds. The birds move to these areas during high tide to avoid disturbance. The offshore islets of Houmet Paradis, Omptolle, La Capelle and the rocks off Fort le Crocq also provide safe and undisturbed roost sites.

Several species of gulls can be found on the beaches and offshore reefs. A resting area at Vazon has had up to 200 **great black-backed gulls** present. **Common terns** nest on several of the offshore islets, (eg Omptolle), and use the bays for feeding. **Rock pipits** and **sand martins** nest amongst the rocky outcrops and banks. The intertidal zone and inshore waters, especially in the sheltered bays of Vazon, Pembroke, Grande Havre, Belle Greve and Perelle to Rocquaine, provide refuge and feeding for several marine species especially divers, grebes and sea-duck. The prevailing weather conditions determine the actual distribution of birds.

Conservation issues
The coastline is under threat from land reclamation and marina development. On a smaller scale there is an increasing demand for leisure and recreational activities. The greater use of jet-skis and sailboards is an obvious example. The great variation in the habitat type means that individual areas have very different conservation problems. These need to be addressed and each area assessed on its own merits as well as being a constituent part of the Guernsey shoreline.

05G   BELLE GREVE BAY
OS Sheet: Guernsey.   Grid Ref: WV340800   **Area:100ha.**

An intertidal area of rock, shingle and sand. At high tide a large sheltered bay protected from the prevailing south-west winds.

Site description
The site includes the large intertidal area extending southwards from St Sampsons to St Peter Port. It is completely built up on the landward side and is being eroded by development at both ends. There is a continuous stretch of intertidal habitat backed against shingle beaches, with hard sea defences preventing any further erosion of the land.

Birds
The large tidal range creates a wide variety of habitats for many species. In addition a long sea sewage outfall creates a nutrient-rich environment which increases the availability of many invertebrate prey species. There are many low-lying rocks and reefs which are used for roosting by gulls and waders. Over 100 **turnstones** are present in early winter. This is over 10% of the total wintering population in the island. The areas of mud and sand are used as feeding grounds for **ringed plover** (50), **oystercatcher** (75) and **grey plover** (35). The sheltered bay has been the prime site in Guernsey for **great crested grebes** with flocks of up to 15 birds being seen. Divers and sea duck are also regular winter visitors to this area.

Conservation issues
The development at both the northern and southern ends of the bay has reduced the area available and increased the pressure on the remaining habitat. There have been schemes to in-fill the whole area although these are not being pursued for the time being. The site provides valuable recreational and leisure opportunities for a densely populated area of the island. The channel between Guernsey and Herm is used extensively by sea traffic. A serious pollution incident could have an immediate and detrimental effect.

06G   GRAND HAVRE, VALE
OS Sheet: Guernsey.   Grid Ref: WV330830.   **Area: 100ha.**

A large natural bay with several sandy beaches. A freshwater outlet from the Vale Pond runs into the bay.

Site description
Formerly the western end of the Braye du Valle, this channel separated the northern Clos du Valle from the rest of Guernsey. The reclamation of the Braye du Valle formed the bay. Extensive areas of mud and sand are exposed at low tide. The narrow entrance to the bay

provides a very good natural harbour for local boats. Rocky outcrops and reefs provide additional shelter during adverse weather conditions.

Birds

The beaches and intertidal zone are used by many shorebirds for feeding and bathing. Both **ringed plover** and **sanderling** flocks number over 50 birds in late winter. This site also has smaller numbers of **dunlin, turnstone** and **grey plover. Common terns** have attempted to breed on at least one of the larger rocky islands in the middle of the bay. **Herring** and **lesser black-backed gulls** use the freshwater stream to bathe in. A roost of over 250 **black-headed gulls** is present in winter. The sheltered area in the centre of the bay provides calmer conditions during rough weather. **Great northern diver, goosander** and **eider** have all been seen in recent years. **Red-necked grebes** have wintered in the bay on several occasions.

Conservation issues

The area is extensively used in summer and winter. Bait digging creates disturbance at low tide. There are at least three mooring sites in the bay and the boat traffic associated with this passes through the central bay. There has been an increase in the cultivation of shellfish and this intrudes into the bay. The possible creation of a barrage across the mouth of the bay to utilise tidal power has been suggested on several occasions.

07G   FORT LE CROCQ, ST. SAVIOUR
OS Sheet: Guernsey.   Grid Ref: WV269797.   **Area: 25ha.**

A west coast rocky headland with several sandy areas and off-lying islands.

Site description

The area lies immediately to the south of Vazon Bay. The rocky foreshore and connected sandy areas form a mosaic of habitats which allows feeding and roosting birds, especially waders, to be undisturbed. The area accumulates considerable amounts of seaweed which attracts many species to feed on the invertebrate fauna that this supports. The rocky platforms and reefs allow other species to roost especially during high tide. The shallow bay and extensive area of sand at low water is rich in marine life. This in turn provides feeding for many species of birds.

Birds

This is the premier site in Guernsey for waders with 22 species having been seen. The birds move to this area to roost when their feeding grounds have been covered. **Turnstones** and **dunlins** can be seen each with flocks of up to 170 birds present in January and February. The islands offshore provide valuable roosting sites for **curlew, grey plover, grey heron** and **little egret**. During migration many other species stop over for varying periods. **Whimbrel** and **bar-tailed godwit** can be present with flocks of over 50 birds passing through especially at peak migration time. Smaller numbers often stay for several days feeding amongst the shingle beach to the south. A feature in late summer is the presence of adult and immature terns. Some will be local birds whilst others must have come from Continental Europe and Britain.

Conservation issues

The advantage of this site is that it is relatively free from disturbance, although shore fishing at high tide may now be becoming a significant disturbance to roosting waders. There is some bait digging but this is minor at the present time. The tipping of hardcore material by a local landowner, in an attempt to prevent erosion of the headland, has been haphazard and incongruous. The area should be considered as a whole with efforts made to co-ordinate policy. External disturbance from jet-skis and boats should be avoided.

Guernsey - Sites of Channel Islands Importance for Birds

which do not meet the criteria for IBA status

Wetland Sites

Wooded Inland Valleys

Lihou Island

Wetland Sites

08G   PULIAS POND, VALE
OS Sheet: Guernsey.   Grid Ref: WV 314829.   **Area: 1ha.**

A small brackish pond with *Phragmites* reed and scrub.

Site description
This shallow tidal pond which is adjacent to the main coast road is one of the few brackish areas of water on the island. The area is immediately behind a storm beach and receives an ingress of sea water at high tide. *Phragmites* reeds have been introduced into the eastern end of the pond and are expanding slowly around the northern shore. The margins consist of mud and shingle. There are several large rocks which provide perching sites for a number of bird species.

Birds
The site is important for passage waders with records of **common sandpiper, ruff** and **little stint** most autumns. In addition the pond provides a sheltered feeding area for **little egret** during strong winds.

Conservation issues
The site is subject to a high level of disturbance from people driving and/or walking along the coast path which overlooks the pond on the seaward side. The continuing growth of *Phragmites* reed should be monitored to check their spread. The small size of the area leaves it vulnerable to in-filling.

09G   VINGTAINE DE L'EPINE, VALE
OS Sheet: Guernsey.   Grid Ref: WV 311814.   **Area: 19ha.**

Wet meadow subject to seasonal flooding.

Site description
An extensive area of grassland with culverted streams. Some small areas of scrub and hedgerow. The site becomes waterlogged in late autumn and shallow areas of standing water are formed. Summer grazing keeps the vegetation short. Some grass is taken for silage. The drier areas are used by Scout and Guide groups for camping and other recreational purposes. The wetter areas attract ducks and wading birds especially during the winter months.

Birds
The inland nature of the site and the fact that it is surrounded by built up areas increases its attraction to birds. An 'oasis' effect is created with several species occurring which one would not associate with the suburban surroundings. **Snipe** and **jack snipe** frequent the wet areas in winter. Other wading birds include **curlew** and **lapwing** as well as

sandpipers and plovers on migration. The area has had **pintail** and **teal** as well as **brent goose**.

Conservation issues

Any extension of residential and developed areas on the boundaries would have a detrimental effect. There are corridors which allow birds uninterrupted passage and provides them with clear fields of view for safety. The main drainage channel has been canalised and is effectively sterile for wildlife. Further drainage is being carried out which will be detrimental. The area is close to a local school and with sympathetic management could provide an excellent teaching resource.

10G   VALE MARAIS, VALE (Marais Nord)
OS Sheet: Guernsey. Grid Ref: WV340832   **Area: 12ha.**

A freshwater pond of significant size, surrounded by small areas of reeds and willow carr. Two unimproved wet meadows adjacent to the area provide additional valuable habitat.

Site description

Formerly just a small part of a very much larger marshy area, the Vale Marais is an important habitat for birds and other fauna and flora. In the late 1960s the present lake (about 3 acres) was excavated. It is now surrounded by a fringe of *Phragmites* reed, with banks lined with willow. Several small thickets of willow remain, and some small mixed copses have been planted. The southern field is used for seasonal grazing, with a significant area remaining flooded well into the spring each year. The western field is a wet unimproved meadow with good populations of loose-flowered and southern marsh orchids and ragged robin. The whole area is currently in the ownership of four separate inhabitants although the lake, most of the willow carr and the reed-bed fall in the same land parcel.

Birds

This site has been well studied: see Vale Marais Reports 1 to 5 covering the period 1971-1992 (*Veron 1971-1992*). It provides an important breeding site for a population of **reed warblers** (about 20 pairs). Other breeding birds include small numbers of **chiffchaff**, **cuckoo**, **mistle thrush**, **coot** and **moorhen**. In winter and during passage the lake is important for wildfowl (19 species recorded), while the flooded fields are excellent for **snipe** with a maximum daily count in excess of 100 birds in many years. In recent years wintering **coot** have reduced very markedly from around 100 to 10 birds per winter. **Moorhen** still winter in good numbers with up to 80 birds present. Ringing studies have shown that the majority of these birds breed in continental Europe. The site is also excellent for freshwater passage waders and is a very important staging post for migrating passerines including in particular **chiffchaff**, **willow warbler**, **sedge** and **reed warblers**, **sand martins** and **swallows**. This is one of the best overall sites remaining in Guernsey and to date has produced no less than 161 species; scarce and/or rare birds being annual.

Conservation issues

The land is currently privately owned by four individuals with the majority being in the hands of one very conservation-minded individual who has taken active steps to improve the area for wildlife. The southern fields remain in agricultural use and while the current owner and tenant are sympathetic to the value of retaining the flooded areas, the needs of running a successful farm are likely to predominate. The western field is also in sympathetic ownership, but the area referred to needs more active management to safeguard the orchid population. The whole surrounding area has been subjected to a high degree of drainage; indeed a major pumping station is located in the southern fields. Any further drainage could be very detrimental. Water pollution has been a problem in the past with high nitrate levels. The lake has also suffered high levels of avian botulism in some years, resulting in the deaths of many wild birds as well as the wildfowl collection birds.

11G   VALE POND, VALE (COLIN McCATHIE NATURE RESERVE)
OS Sheet: Guernsey.   Grid Ref: WV334824.   Area: 5ha.

The largest area of brackish water in the island. Fringed with reeds and subject to tidal influence, this is another of the most important ornithological sites in the island.

Site description

The last remnant of the Braye du Valle which originally separated Guernsey into two islands. The Braye was reclaimed in 1808. The channel which separated the Clos du Valle from the main island was formerly an area of salt pans and marsh. An embankment across the western end and the construction of drainage channels allowed the vast majority of the area to be reclaimed. The pond that remains is the main focus for drainage over a considerable area. The area is leased to La Société Guernesiaise, and extensive maintenance and enhancement work has been carried out in recent years. The reeds and scrub provide breeding habitat for an important variety of species. The muddy margins are frequented by waders and other waterfowl. In addition to the pond area the grassland to the east is often used as a roost site by ducks, waders and gulls.

Birds

The large variety of species, over 140 of which have been recorded at the Vale Pond, is proof of its attraction to birds. The regular passage of waders including **whimbrel**, **greenshank** and **common sandpiper** can also include **avocet** and **black-tailed godwit**. In addition to being an important breeding site for **reed warbler** and **moorhen**,the reeds are used by migrating **reed** and **sedge warblers** as well as being roosting sites for **swallows** and **sand martins**. The winter brings many species of duck and good numbers of **snipe** and **lapwing**. If the island is acting as a refuge during hard weather elsewhere in Western Europe, then the whole area can be filled with birds.

Conservation issues

Although the area is under sympathetic management there are a number of issues which could have an impact in conservation terms. The water flowing through the pond could be a source of water-borne pollution. The build up of nitrates or an accidental spillage of chemicals would immediately feed into the pond's ecosystem. In addition the silt that is deposited needs to be removed regularly to preserve the open water. The wet meadow areas on the eastern side need to be included in any planning considerations as well as the fields that allow an open approach from the south. Already one of the most popular sites for bird-watching in Guernsey with both locals and visitors, the potential as an attraction is obvious.

12G   ST SAVIOUR'S RESERVOIR, ST SAVIOUR
OS Sheet: Guernsey. Grid Ref: WV275782.   **Area: 25ha.**

The largest surface area of freshwater on the island. This is one of the two major sources of drinking water for the island's population.

Site description
An extensive area of open water surrounded by conifer and deciduous plantations. The margins are gently shelving in many areas which allows some species to utilise this habitat. This contrasts with the majority of the quarries in the island which have steep rock walls which are unsuitable for most birds. The wooded surrounds form an effective barrier and consequently there is little disturbance. The whole site lies in a predominately agricultural area and the open water provides roosting and bathing for many of the gulls which feed on the fields. There is considerable fluctuation in the water level and this provides an additional feeding area for certain species.

Birds
The open water is attractive to several species of diving duck, eg **pochard, goldeneye** and **tufted duck**, especially in winter. During migration the muddy areas provide feeding for waders including **green sandpiper, greenshank** and **common sandpiper**. There are often sizeable flocks of hirundines, ie **swallows** and **martins,** hunting insects over the site during migration passages of these birds. The wooded areas provide feeding and breeding habitat for several species including **chiffchaff, blackcap** and **spotted flycatcher**. The conifer plantation has had breeding **firecrest** in some years. Although it has not been conclusively proved, it is suspected that **kingfishers** may summer and could breed if conditions were right. **Little grebes** have summered and again could breed.

Conservation issues
There is always pressure to allow increased access to the site. The present arrangements which permit only small numbers of trout fishermen to use the reservoir obviously works well. They act as wardens and require an undisturbed site to carry on their activities. Water-borne pollution is strictly monitored by the States Water Board in view of the vital importance to safeguard the island's water supply.

13G   LA GRANDE MARE, CASTEL
OS Sheet: Guernsey. Grid Ref: WV586796.   **Area: 50ha.**

A large open low-lying area which was formerly an extensive marsh. The site has been considerably altered during the construction of a 14 hole golf course. Some pockets of the former habitat survive although these are fragmented and small in size.

Site description
La Grande Mare was formerly a large marshy area lying just inland from Vazon Bay on

the West Coast. It receives the water from the escarpment to the east as well as the considerable stream flowing down the Fauxquets Valley. The area used to provide summer grazing but was too wet during the winter. There were some extensive areas of willow scrub which have almost all been removed. Large scale landscaping has altered the appearance and there is a much greater variation in levels than previously was the case. The rough grazing and sward has been replaced with standard golf course grasses which are regularly cut. A number of additional water areas have been incorporated although these are more ornamental than practical from an ornithological point of view.

Birds

The past bird records from La Grande Mare are unfortunately unlikely to provide much help in assessing what the site in its present form will attract. There are still some areas suitable for breeding **reed warblers** and it may be that these will provide a nucleus from which the species will expand. Wintering birds, eg gulls and waders, continue to use the area whenever the human disturbance is not too great.

Conservation issues

The Planning Inquiry which considered the development of the area recommended that certain areas be out of bounds for construction of the golf course. This may not be sufficient as the surrounding areas will be subject to alteration and increased activity. The main area is undergoing a significant tree planting scheme which will further dry out the area. There are several areas of importance from a nature conservation point of view. The developers of the golf course still require additional land to permit eventually an 18 hole course to be constructed. Those sites of scientific importance which constrict the development will be under the greatest threat.

14G   LES LANDES, VALE (Le Grand Pré)
OS Sheet: Guernsey.   Grid Ref: WV350832. 　　　　　　　**Area: 5ha.**

A modestly sized area of *Phragmites* reed with pools of standing water.

Site description

One of the few remaining fragments of a once extensive area of reed and marsh. The peaty soil retains considerable volumes of water which have allowed the development of a reed bed. The area also has some open rough grassland and in addition recent management work has created a series of pools with standing water. The site was not maintained for many years; this resulted in parts drying out so much so that reed growth was inhibited. The main area is now under management by La Société Guernesiaise and attempts are being made to encourage the regrowth of *Phragmites* reed and to increase the retention of water during the summer months.

Birds

An important site for breeding **reed warblers** and migrating birds especially **reed** and **sedge warblers**. This was formerly an excellent location for **Cetti's warbler** but the severe winters in the mid and late eighties have extirpated this population. If the species attempts recolonisation then the area would be ideal. **Bearded tits** have been recorded and this site could provide suitable breeding habitat in the future. Up to 100 **snipe** regularly winter on the area.

Conservation issues

The area was formerly much larger. Some parts may be vulnerable to in-filling as there are several landowners involved. The States of Guernsey own the greater part of the area. The site is surrounded by residential and horticultural property. There could be concern that the land may be perceived as being 'derelict' and should therefore be 'improved.' The increasing fragmentation and reduction in size of these pockets of undeveloped land increases their isolation. This makes the movement between sites by foraging birds more difficult.

15G   L'ERÉE (including LA CLAIRE MARE), ST. PIERRE DU BOIS
OS Sheet: Guernsey.   Grid Ref: WV255785.   **Area: 50ha.**

Open low-lying grassland with drainage ditches. An area of open water and *Phragmites* forms the northern boundary. One extensive reed bed is still present.

Site description

A large open area lying just inland from the coast. There are three distinct types of habitat. The first is the grassland. This is grazed by sheep and is occasionally used as an arena for various public events. There are a number of wet areas which have suffered from the tipping of hardcore and rubble. Many birds feed and roost in the fields which, because of the openness of the site, provides security from predators. The reed beds at the northern edge of the site are some of the largest of this habitat type left in the Island. In addition there are willow and tamarisk hedges which provide additional cover. La Société Guernesiaise has created an area of open water (La Claire Mare) which attracts passage waders and water birds. The former low-lying fields have been dug out to ensure that water is retained. Control of the stream flow allows the water level to be altered as required.

Birds

The fields are used as both a roost and feeding ground with some species recorded in high numbers eg up to 140 **curlew**. This is the largest wintering flock in the island. A number of other species including **whimbrel, bar-tailed godwit** and **redshank** feed in the grassy areas. In addition to the feeding birds, other species use the site for resting especially at high tide when coastal roosts are too exposed. Up to 40 **grey herons** and over 150 **great black-backed gulls** have been recorded. The reed beds attract migrant warblers, and these include the internationally threatened **aquatic warbler** in autumn. **Swallows** and martins roost as well as **pied** and **yellow wagtails**. At least one pair of **reed buntings** still frequent the site, this being one of the few remaining breeding locations in Guernsey. The open water and exposed muddy margins of La Claire Mare provide valuable feeding for migrant and wintering birds. **Snipe** and **jack snipe** occur in winter and up to 14 species of wader have been seen on passage. The number of wildfowl using the site is increasing. This should continue as the area matures.

Conservation issues

The primary land use of the grassland area is agricultural. There have been attempts to improve the land with low-lying areas being filled in. This reduces the attraction for wading birds. The occasional use for public events could become so regular that the site is completely disturbed and so prevent the birds from using the area. The reedbeds are non-productive for the land owner and could be eliminated for commercial reasons. Hedges and scrub areas could be removed. The land owned by La Société Guernesiaise could be isolated by alterations to the drainage in the area. The water levels need to be controlled to preserve the habitat.

16G   ST SAMPSON'S MARAIS, ST SAMPSON
OS Sheet: Guernsey.   Grid Ref: WV335806.   **Area: 50ha.**

A large unimproved low-lying area just inland from the east coast. Subject to seasonal flooding, the area was formerly an extensive reed bed. Only a fraction of the original habitat survives.

Site description
Surrounded by developed areas, the site remains one of the largest open habitats in Guernsey. A number of hedges and dry stone walls provide links between various habitats. The grassland tends to be heavily grazed by cattle which reduces the attractiveness for birds. A small area of *Phragmites* still exists and this would regenerate if allowed to. During autumn and winter parts become waterlogged and standing water is present. The whole site is a mosaic of different habitats which is unusual for the island. The undeveloped agricultural land and adjacent playing fields provide additional open areas.

Birds
A site for passage waders and waterfowl. The ducks include **garganey**, **teal** and **pintail**. **Ruff**, **greenshank** and **green sandpiper** are regular on passage. The numbers of these species fluctuate year to year. Many pipits and wagtails are present in spring and autumn. In winter **fieldfares** and other thrushes can be found feeding on the overgrown hedges.

Conservation issues
The site lies immediately between the two most developed areas in the island. This puts considerable pressure on the land. There has already been considerable degradation of the site with a large drainage channel having been installed. Some development has already occurred with the building of the new prison.

Wooded Inland Valleys

17G   WOODED INLAND VALLEYS
OS Sheet: Guernsey.   Grid Ref: See below.

A variety of mixed woodland habitat.

Site description
The areas are restricted to valley sides which are too difficult to farm. Most were either planted by man or consist of self-sown secondary woodland. The dominant species are pedunculate oak, ash, sycamore, Guernsey elm and hybrid Guernsey elm. The shrub layer is mainly holly, hawthorn, blackthorn, elder or sallow. The more important valleys are:

FAUXQUETS VALLEY, CATEL, ST ANDREWS. WV 293785 to WV 299772. Area: 27ha.

The largest single wooded area on the island. Important for **sparrowhawk** and other diurnal raptors. Part of the valley is managed as a conservation area.

TALBOT VALLEY, CATEL/ST ANDREW. WV 294786 to WV 301782. Area: 46ha.

Adjacent to above area providing additional wooded habitat. There is more open ground and the site is regularly used by hunting **barn owls**.

HAVILLAND/FOULON, ST ANDREW. WV322780 to WV 322788. Area: 20ha.

An area on the edge of the developed areas of St Peter Port. The largest part is private but it links to the Foulon/Dell Nursery which have many mature trees. It provides an important route from the central wooded area to the east coast.

PETIT BÔT, FOREST/ST MARTIN. WV 300752 to WV 308754. Area: 18ha.

South facing valley running to coast. Important for migrant passerines.

FERMAIN/BOUVÉE, ST PETER PORT/ST MARTIN. WV 332762 to WV 339769 and WV 337755 to WV 340755. Area: 11ha.

Small east facing valleys on coast. Breeding **long-eared owl** and **sparrowhawk**.

SILBE/LA RUE DES VINAIRES, ST PIERRE DU BOIS. WV 263765 to WV 265767. Area: 10ha.

Two small valleys running inland from Rocquaine. There is still a fair amount of tree and scrub cover. Open woodland and woodland edge species are present in both valleys.

Birds

The areas provide breeding sites for a variety of species which are typically found in broad-leaved deciduous habitat which is scarce elsewhere on the island. **Short-toed treecreepers** are resident in all the areas and the three species of **tits - great, blue** and **long-tailed** - which breed on the island occur in good numbers. **Garden warbler** and **blackcap** tend to favour the edges of these wooded areas. A number of unusual species have summered in these valleys which may be a prelude to future colonisation. **Golden orioles** and **great spotted woodpecker** have both stayed in the Fauxquets Valley in spring and a pair of **firecrest** successfully raised young in the past three years. The recent recolonisation by **sparrowhawks** has centred on the inland sites. They also provide feeding areas for large numbers of spring and autumn migrants which pass through the island. These include several species of warblers and chats which accumulate fat deposits before continuing their migrations.

Conservation issues

All the areas suffer from disturbance to some degree. There is a clay pigeon shooting range located in one of the valleys which creates substantial disturbance when in use. Motor cycle scrambling takes place during the winter at several locations. The fragmentation of the sites means that the small populations are becoming isolated and so are vulnerable to elimination.

18G LIHOU ISLAND
OS Sheet: Guernsey. Grid Ref: WV242790   **Area: 16ha.**

A small island isolated from Guernsey at high tide. Connected at low tide by a man-made causeway.

Site description
Situated off the west coast of Guernsey this was formerly a private island with limited public access. A large house and associated outbuildings dominate the eastern side. The remainder of the island is covered in bracken and rough grass. Shingle and pebble beaches together with the exposed causeway provide additional habitat.

Birds
A major high tide roost site for waders and gulls with **oystercatcher** (350) and **herring gull** (500). The area is used by up to 25 **little egrets.** In addition the shingle areas provide nesting habitat for **ringed plover, oystercatcher** and, in some years, **common terns**. A few pairs of **shags** breed on the two small islets (Lihoumel 1 and 2) which are connected to Lihou at low tide. The island is also an important refuge for migrant passerines.

Conservation issues
Recently acquired by the States of Guernsey, this is a unique site which is important for archeological and historical reasons. There is tremendous potential for educational purposes. There is a high level of human disturbance in summer. The numbers of people visiting the island are causing erosion in some areas. A warden has been appointed to study the area.

Alderney - Important Bird Areas
which meet the criteria for IBA status

Heathlands (Alderney Heathland IBA) composed of:

Seabird colonies

Heathlands

01A   LE GIFFOINE
OS Sheet: Alderney. Grid Ref: WA557066.   **Area: 63ha. (approx.)**

Coastal heath on the west end of Alderney, dominated by heather, gorse and scrub, but with bracken invasion. This site has held breeding Dartford warblers.

Site description
A small but valuable area of coastal heath dominated by heather and gorse, with areas of blackthorn and bramble scrub.

Birds
The area has held resident **Dartford warblers**. In the period 1973-84 this area, combined with the heathlands at Trois Vaux, supported c. 15 pairs of **Dartford warbler** (2.5% of British and C.I. population). Since the harsh winters of 1984/85, 1985/86 and 1986/87, however, there have been no breeding records. In more recent years **Dartford warblers** have been recorded again during the summer and recolonisation is expected.

Conservation issues
Threats to the heathland include agricultural land-claim, invasions of bracken and lack of management, especially of gorse.

02A   TROIS VAUX
OS Sheet: Alderney.   Grid Ref: WA590073.   **Area: 30ha. (approx.)**

Coastal heath on the south coast of Alderney, dominated by heather and gorse. This site has held breeding Dartford warblers.

Site description
A small but valuable area of coastal heath dominated by heather and gorse, with areas of bracken and scrub.

Birds
Along with the above site (Le Giffoine) Trois Vaux has held resident **Dartford warblers**. Although the species has not bred since the harsh winters in the late 1980s, birds have been seen again in recent summers and autumns, and recolonisation is expected.

Conservation issues
Threats to the heathland include invasions of bracken and lack of management, especially of gorse.

Seabird Colonies

03A   LES ÉTACS (The Garden Rocks)
OS Sheet: Alderney. Grid Ref. WA550062.   **Area: 0.6ha.**

(Note: This site is included with Ortac as Channel Islands site 001 in the European IBA book).

Several small igneous offshore rocks.

Site description
A small group of several igneous rocks rising to 39 metres above sea-level, lying 200 metres off the west coast of Alderney. There is virtually no vegetation cover.

Birds
The principal interest is the breeding **gannets**. The colony began in the 1940s. With the exception of Rouzic in the Sept-Îles off the coast of Brittany, this is the southernmost colony of **gannets** in the eastern Atlantic. By 1946 the colony had grown to c 200 pairs (*Dobson & Lockley 1946*); with 1,010 pairs in 1960; 2,000 pairs in 1969 (*Cramp et al 1974*); 2,810 pairs (2% of British and C.I. population) (*Hill 1990*) and 3,380 pairs in 1994 (*Hill - pers. comm.*). It is still expanding.

There is a control of a nestling ringed on Les Étacs breeding at a newly established breeding colony in northern Norway. Other recoveries suggest emigration to colonies in Scotland.

Conservation issues
Much nylon rope and fishing line is found among gannet nests and this causes the death of a number of birds, both adults and nestlings, every year. However as the colony is still expanding this does not appear to have much effect on the total number of breeding birds.

04A   ORTAC
Lat: 49°43' 27" N. Long: 20°17' 30" W.   **Area: 0.1ha.**

(Note: This site is included with Les Etacs as Channel Islands site 001 in the European IBA book).

A small isolated sandstone stack.

Site description
A single Cambrian sandstone rock rising 24 metres above sea-level. It is located 4.5 km off the north-west coast of Alderney. There is virtually no vegetation.

Birds

The rock is of importance as a significant gannetry. Colonisation began in about 1940. It had expanded to c 250 pairs in 1946 (*Dobson & Lockley 1946*); 925 pairs in 1960; 1,000 pairs in 1969 (*Cramp et al 1974*); 2,106 pairs (1% of British and C.I. population) by 1989 (*Hill, 1990*). It is now probably at capacity. There is a control of a nestling ringed on Ortac in 1989, breeding at a newly established breeding colony in northern Norway in 1996.

Conservation issues

Discarded nylon fishing nets and ropes, which are used by gannets in their nest-building, snare and kill adult and nestling birds every year. However this does not appear to be reducing the breeding population.

Alderney - Sites of Channel Islands Importance for Birds
which do not meet the criteria for IBA status

The Alderney group of islands which are part of the Bailiwick of Guernsey lie about 10km west of Cap de la Hague on the westernmost point of Normandy and 30 km north-east of Guernsey. The population of about 2,000 relies largely on tourism, fishing and financial services for its living. In describing the sites of Channel Island Importance for Birds the areas have been divided into Alderney Mainland and the island of Burhou, including Renoquet Reef and Les Casquets Rock. They are all important for their breeding seabirds. The main island also provides important habitats for migrating birds.

05A   ALDERNEY MAINLAND
OS Sheet: Alderney. Grid Ref: WA575075.   **Area: 10km² (approx.)**

Site description
The island is about 6 km long by 2 km wide and rises to a height of approx. 85m. The north and part of the south coasts are low and rocky with some adjacent dune slacks. The remainder of the south coast and the short west coast consist of rugged granite cliffs. The island is windswept with few trees except in sheltered valleys and gardens.

Birds
Virtually all the important colonies of seabirds breeding occur on the cliffs and offshore islets of the south-west corner. They comprise 40 pairs of **fulmar**, 200 pairs of **shag**, 55 pairs of **lesser black-backed gulls** and 95 pairs of **kittiwake**. In addition there are 170 **guillemot**, 80 **razorbill** and about 50 **puffin** nesting on the islets which lie just off the south-west corner. The only exception is the 30 pairs of **common tern** which nest on the low islands off the north-east corner. In addition a small number of **oystercatchers** breed on the islets off the north-west coast. **Peregrine falcons** are once again regular and are probably breeding on the cliffs at the western end of the island.

In addition to having impressive breeding seabirds, Alderney is very strategically positioned to host migratory species at both seasons. It has the best raptor passage of any of the Channel Islands and 'falls' of passerines can be very impressive. In view of the small size of the island, and its largely rural character outside the main developed area of St Anne's, the Banquage and the harbour, the greater part of the island should be regarded as being important for birds.

Particularly good areas include the cliff top and heathland from the Giffoine to the airport and beyond to Fort Essex, the northern dune system, sheltered wooded valleys on the south coast and at Barrack Masters' Lane and Val de la Bonne Terre. Mannez Quarry in the north provides water for wildfowl, while the surrounding scrub holds migrant passerines including **common whitethroat, redstart, willow warbler, chiffchaff, whinchat** and **wheatear**. The best bays for wintering grebes and passage birds are Braye Bay, Longy Bay and Longy Marsh, while Saline Bay was the last known breeding site for **Kentish plover** in the Channel Islands. It currently has breeding **ringed plovers**.

Conservation issues

While the States of Alderney require any person wishing to land on any offshore islet in the breeding season to have a special permit, this has no legal status. At present the system appears to work very well in the small community of Alderney, but it may need to be reviewed in future.

In July 1996 the States of Alderney amended their wild bird protection legislation to allow for the culling of any wild bird species on the grounds of public nuisance through the removal of eggs. Conservation bodies regard this as a development of concern on several counts; including the fact that scientific data played no part in the decision making process of the Government, that the law could be open to abuse, and that it could be used against any wild bird species. The conservation bodies contend that if any licences are issued under this legislation the details should be made known and the effects of any action taken should be monitored scientifically.

The other main issue relates to the inadequate habitat protection legislation to conserve and enhance key ecosystems. Although Alderney has attracted study from excellent amateur naturalists, it is inevitable that in such a small community there are areas where scientific information is lacking to identify, and provide the objective data required, to protect key areas.

While Alderney has clustered its housing development together, leaving the greater part of the island with a very rural character, pressure to develop into more 'green' sites may grow in future.

06A   BURHOU, RENONQUET REEF AND LES CASQUESTS
Lat: 49°43'27"N Long: 02°17'30"W   Area: 30ha. (approx.)

Site description

Burhou island, 5 km to the north of Alderney, is about 1 km long and about half a km wide. It is a low island with a rocky shoreline and is covered with bracken and low turf. About 2 km to the west of Burhou is the Renonquet reef and further west, also about 2 km, is Les Casquets rock where there is an unmanned lighthouse.

Birds

Although at one time the population of **storm petrels** on Burhou might have been well over 1,000 pairs, the current population is estimated to be about 150 pairs. The 275 pairs of **lesser black-backed gulls** on Burhou represent an important colony for the

Channel Islands as a whole. In addition a further 40 pairs of **great black–backed gulls** nest on Burhou and its offshore islands. At one time several thousand **puffins** nested on Burhou. Now the figure is estimated to be about 300.

Conservation issues

The island is rat-free and designated a nature reserve by the States of Alderney. Landings are prohibited except by permit until the second half of July each year. Better control of bracken might lead to more puffin breeding. Further research work to identify the main breeding areas of storm petrel may also assist in minimising disturbance to the sites for the extended breeding season of this species. Reference is made earlier in this account to the legislation recently passed to legalise the culling of wild species by the removal of eggs when this is considered to be necessary to avoid public nuisance. The view of the conservation bodies is that part of the debate centred around unfounded and incorrect accusations that "black-backed gulls" were responsible for the decline of puffins on Burhou. These bodies are concerned that legislation can be passed on such spurious grounds and consider that this raises worries which go wider than management issues on Burhou.

Sark - Sites of Channel Islands Importance for Birds
which do not meet the criteria for IBA status

SARK, BRECQHOU AND OFFSHORE ISLETS

Sark and its offshore islands and islets, including Brecqhou, lie 12 km east of Guernsey and 35 km from the west coast of the Cotentin peninsula in Normandy. Although part of the Bailiwick of Guernsey, Sark has its own parliament called Chief Pleas, which is presided over by the Seigneur. It has a population of about 600 but there is a large influx of tourists, particularly day visitors, in the spring and summer. It is best divided into three sections: Big Sark and Little Sark which are joined by a very narrow sheer-sided ridge, and the small island of Brecqhou which is about 400 m to the west of Big Sark. It is important for its breeding seabirds and for the passerines which use the island to rest and feed during spring and autumn passage.

01S   BIG SARK
Lat: 49°26'00"N Long: 02°21'30"W   **Area: 7km². (approx.)**

Site description

Big Sark is basically a plateau about 90 m high rising out of the sea from granite cliffs. It is about 4.5 km long by 3.5 km wide. The less steep slopes at the top of the cliffs are covered with bracken, gorse or scrub consisting mostly of hawthorn or blackthorn. There are a number of islets off both the east and west coasts, some covered in low vegetation.

Birds

Most of the total of about 30 pairs of **fulmar** breed on the steep cliffs of the west coast. There is a small colony of possibly 10 pairs of **Manx shearwater** on the north-east coast. About 40 pairs of **shag** nest on the offshore islets off the east coast. Of the gulls the most important are the 300 pairs of **lesser black-backed gulls** which nest on the coasts and offshore islets. The largest colony of **guillemot** in the whole of the Channel Islands is on Les Autelets off the west coast - 120 individuals. About 40 pairs of **oystercatchers** nest on the offshore islets and on the rocky shore of some of the cliffs. After an interval of several decades a pair of **peregrine falcons** now breeds on the cliffs of the west coast, although they sometimes move their nest-site to the cliffs of Little Sark. Two pairs of

sparrowhawk now breed regularly using sites at Port du Moulin and near the Hogg's Back, and there is one pair of breeding **long-eared owls** near the Harbour hill.

Ringing studies carried out at a site on the north coast (La Fougeraie) have shown that the island's scrub and common land habitats are widely used by significant numbers of migratory birds during both spring and autumn passages. As the island is small and rural in character it is the patchwork of fields, traditional hedgerows, scrub and common land area and the small woodlands and gardens (on both Big and Little Sark) which provides good habitat. Particularly good sites include the Harbour Hill, La Grève de la Ville, La Fougeraie (Banquette), Eperquerie Common, Port du Moulin and Dixcart Valley.

Conservation issues

The small colony of Manx shearwaters has been badly affected by a feral cat. Although Sark has little in the way of laws to protect flora and fauna or their habitats, this does not appear to affect conservation of wildlife to any great degree. As everywhere in the Channel Islands development resulting from the need to build more housing, and changing land-use remain potential threats even in Sark.

02S   LITTLE SARK (INCLUDING L'ÉTAC DE SERK)
Lat: 49°26'00"N Long: 02°22'30"W   **Area: 1.5km². (approx.)**

Site description

Little Sark is separated from Big Sark by a narrow ridge with a road across the top, La Coupée. It is much smaller, being about 2 km by 1 km. It has a resident population of under 50 but a large influx of visitors in the spring and summer. It is surrounded by a number of rocky islets including L'Étac de Serk about 1 km to the south.

Birds

Most of the breeding seabirds on the Little Sark site breed on L'Étac de Serk. They include 80-100 **shag**, 80-100 **guillemot**, 10-15 **razorbill**, about 100 **puffins** and up to 15 pairs of **common tern**. A pair of **cormorant** nest on L'Étac in some years. On Little Sark itself the most interesting colony is that of about 30 **Manx shearwater** on the east coast, but there are also about 30 pairs of **fulmar** on the east coast and 50-60 pairs of **lesser black-backed gulls** on the offshore islets including some on L'Étac de Serk. A colony of about 20 **common tern** breeds sporadically on L'Étac de Serk or the islet of Moie de la Bretagne.

Conservation issues

The same remarks apply as to Big Sark. There is a danger of predation from cats and escaped ferrets at the small Manx shearwater colony on the south-east coast.

03S BRECQHOU
Lat: 49°26'00"N Long: 02°23'50"W   **Area: 60ha. (approx.)**

Site description
Brecqhou is a small island about 1 km in length and slightly less in breadth, lying very close to the west of the west coast of Sark. Generally speaking its cliffs are less steep than those on Sark and it rises to about 60 or 70 m in the centre. It is privately owned. There are relics of farming on the island. It is closed to visitors.

Birds
The principal interest lies in the relatively large colony of **lesser black-backed gulls** – about 330 pairs. In addition there are 60 pairs of **shag**.

Conservation issues
Being privately owned with a very low population there are unlikely to be conservation issues relating to human disturbance etc. Recent developments on the island by new owners did involve a major influx of workmen for several years. This is very likely to have had some detrimental effect in terms of disturbance to breeding birds, but with the building works now being completed this situation has come to an end. However the island was infested by both black and brown rats, although it is believed that attempts have been made to eliminate them. The success of the island's breeding birds relies to a significant extent on the attitude of the particular owner of the island.

Herm, Jethou and Offshore Islets - Sites of Channel Islands Importance for Birds
which do not meet the criteria for IBA status

HERM AND OFFSHORE ISLETS

This group of islands, important for its breeding seabirds, lies some 5 km to the east of St Peter Port Harbour in Guernsey. For the purpose of this book they have been divided into three: Herm and its offshore islets, Jethou and Les Amfroques (known locally as The Humps).

01H   HERM
Lat: 49°28'36"N Long: 2°26'45"W   **Area: 3km² (approx.)**

Site description

Herm is the main island of the group. It is owned by the Crown and administered by the States of Guernsey Board of Administration. It has been leased to a private individual since the end of World War II and the lease has recently been extended up to the year 2025. There are about 50 permanent residents but particularly during the summer months this small population is supplemented by a large number of day visitors, campers and boat owners. The island is about 4 km long by 1 km wide. The southern half consists of granite cliffs rising to about 60 metres. They are either bare rock or have some sparse vegetation. The more level upper areas support a small farm with a number of grass fields and some woodland. There is much bracken, gorse and blackthorn, particularly on the east and west cliffs. The northern part of the island is a complete contrast to the south and consists of sand dunes which are for the most part stabilised. The larger offshore islets have some vegetation while the smaller islets are generally bare rock. Brehon Tower is a substantial Victorian gun emplacement built on a low rock in the Little Russel half-way between Herm and Guernsey.

Birds

The site is primarily of importance for small breeding populations of **puffin** - 30 individuals on the south-east coast, and **common tern** - 50 pairs on Brehon Tower, although the latter do not breed every year probably due to human disturbance. In addition there are small populations of 30 pairs of **fulmar** on the south-east coast, and 20 pairs of **shag**, 30 pairs of **lesser black-backed gulls**, and 10 pairs of **great black-backed gulls** on the offshore islets. On the mainland of Herm there is a wintering population of about 100 **dark-bellied brent geese** based on the north and north-west coasts. In the conifers behind the village area a pair of **long-eared owls** breed. A pair of **ravens** regularly breed on the south coast cliffs and a pair of **ringed plovers** bred on the north coast in 1994. A few pairs of **stonechat** also nest on the common area in the north of the island, and there have been recent sightings of **Dartford warblers** there.

Conservation issues

The laws of Guernsey also apply to Herm. Although the current tenant is conservation-minded, the presence of a resident population and a very large influx of visitors from April onwards must have its effect on the numbers of breeding shore birds. There is obviously little that can be done about this except possibly by roping off one or two areas of sand dune or sandy beach during the breeding season. The Brehon Tower which normally supports a small colony of common terns is disturbed by boat owners who land to explore the Tower and the States of Guernsey have recently prohibited landing before the 15th July each year. The seabirds which nest on the southern cliffs of Herm do not seem to be greatly disturbed by visitors. However, during the spring and summer large numbers of powerboats visit Herm, often travelling at speed through the passage between Herm and Jethou and this inevitably disturbs rafts of birds such as auks which breed in small numbers on the east side of Jethou and the south side of Herm. Speed limits have been imposed in certain areas but these are difficult to police.

02H   JETHOU
Lat: 49°27'45"N Long: 02°27'30"W   **Area: 40ha. (approx.)**

Site description

Jethou is a small roughly circular island about 500m across. It is owned by the Crown but is leased to a private owner. It is steep sided with a partly cultivated plateau and some woodland. The low cliffs of the eastern side have less vegetation. Crevichon to the north of Jethou is conical in form with an old quarry on the east side. Broken rock is scattered over the whole area. Vegetation, mostly bracken, is confined largely to the east side of the island. Grande Fauconnière, off the south coast, is mainly a bare granite rock with little vegetation. Both islands are connected to the main island at low tide.

Birds

The site is of interest for its small breeding populations of **puffins**, 40 individuals, and **Manx shearwaters** (under 10 pairs). In addition there are expanding populations of **shag** (210 pairs) on the two offshore islets and the low cliffs, **lesser black-backed gulls** (55 pairs) mostly on Crevichon, **herring gulls** (150 pairs), half on the main island and half on Crevichon, and **great black-backed gulls** (45 pairs). There is also a small breeding population of **razorbill** (up to 10 individuals) on Grande Fauconnière.

Conservation issues

The island is privately leased. Visitors may only visit after obtaining permission and then normally in organised parties. There is therefore very little human disturbance. There is probably some disturbance to the small breeding colonies of puffins and Manx shearwaters from brown rats but an attempt has been made to control them. In addition the powerboats using the narrow passage between Jethou and Herm tend to disturb auks resting on the water.

03H   LES AMFROQUES ('The Humps')
Lat: 49°29'30"N Long: 02°26'00"W   Area: 4ha. (approx.)

Site description

This group of islands, six in all, lies between one and four km to the north-east of Herm. They consist largely of rocky outcrops, one or two with stony beaches and some with a very small amount of vegetation. The States of Guernsey Board of Administration administers them.

Birds

The Humps are principally of interest for their breeding populations of auks: 120 **guillemots**, 25 **razorbill** and 15 **puffin**. In addition a population of 25 pairs of **cormorant** is the main colony for the whole of the Bailiwick of Guernsey. Other birds of interest are **shag** (120 pairs), **lesser black-backed gulls** (55 pairs), **herring gulls** (55 pairs) and **great black-backed gulls** (40 pairs).

Conservation issues

Generally speaking this small group of islands remains almost completely undisturbed throughout most of the year. However, over the last ten years, with the increase in the number and variety of boats and boatowners, there has been a tendency for people to land on some of the islands, particularly on calm days in the spring and summer months, resulting in some disturbance to breeding birds. The States of Guernsey Board of Administration designated the Humps as a nature reserve in 1990 and erected notice boards asking people not to land on the islands before 15 July each year. This has helped to reduce disturbance and increase breeding success.

APPENDIX 1:
LIST OF BIRD SPECIES MENTIONED IN TEXT

Great Northern Diver	*Gavia immer*
Little Grebe	*Tachybaptus ruficollis*
Great Crested Grebe	*Podiceps cristatus*
Red-necked Grebe	*P. grisegena*
Fulmar	*Fulmarus glacialis*
Manx Shearwater	*Puffinus puffinus*
Storm Petrel	*Hydrobates pelagicus*
Gannet	*Morus bassanus*
Cormorant	*Phalacrocorax carbo*
Shag	*P. aristotelis*
Bittern	*Botaurus stellaris*
Little Egret	*Egretta garzetta*
Grey Heron	*Ardea cinerea*
Brent Goose	*Branta bernicla*
Teal	*Anas crecca*
Pintail	*A. acuta*
Garganey	*A. querquedula*
Shoveler	*A. clypeata*
Pochard	*Aythya ferina*
Tufted Duck	*A. fuligula*
Eider	*Somateria mollissima*
Goldeneye	*Bucephala clangula*
Goosander	*Mergus merganser*
Marsh Harrier	*Circus aeruginosus*
Hen Harrier	*C. cyaneus*
Sparrowhawk	*Accipiter nisus*
Kestrel	*Falco tinnunculus*
Merlin	*F. columbarius*
Peregrine	*F. peregrinus*
Moorhen	*Gallinula chloropus*
Coot	*Fulica atra*
Oystercatcher	*Haematopus ostralegus*
Avocet	*Recurvirostra avosetta*
Stone-curlew	*Burhinus oedicnemus*
Ringed Plover	*Charadrius hiaticula*
Kentish Plover	*C. alexandrinus*
Dotterel	*C. morinellus*
Golden Plover	*Pluvialis apricaria*
Grey Plover	*P. squatarola*
Lapwing	*Vanellus vanellus*
Sanderling	*Calidris alba*

Little Stint	*C. minuta*
Dunlin	*C. alpina*
Buff-breasted Sandpiper	*Tryngites subruficollis*
Ruff	*Philomachus pugnax*
Jack Snipe	*Lymnocryptes minimus*
Snipe	*Gallinago gallinago*
Black-tailed Godwit	*Limosa limosa*
Bar-tailed Godwit	*L. lapponica*
Whimbrel	*Numenius phaeopus*
Curlew	*N. arquata*
Redshank	*Tringa totanus*
Greenshank	*T. nebularia*
Green Sandpiper	*T. ochropus*
Common Sandpiper	*Actitis hypoleucos*
Turnstone	*Arenaria interpres*
Little Gull	*Larus minutus*
Black-headed Gull	*L. ridibundus*
Lesser Black-backed Gull	*L. fuscus*
Herring Gull	*L. argentatus*
Great Black-backed Gull	*L. marinus*
Kittiwake	*Rissa tridactyla*
Common Tern	*Sterna hirundo*
Guillemot	*Uria aalge*
Razorbill	*Alca torda*
Puffin	*Fratercula arctica*
Cuckoo	*Cuculus canorus*
Barn Owl	*Tyto alba*
Long-eared Owl	*Asio otus*
Short-eared Owl	*A. flammeus*
Nightjar	*Caprimulgus europaeus*
Swift	*Apus apus*
Kingfisher	*Alcedo atthis*
Wryneck	*Jynx torquilla*
Great Spotted Woodpecker	*Dendrocopos major*
Lesser Spotted Woodpecker	*D. minor*
Skylark	*Alauda arvensis*
Sand Martin	*Riparia riparia*
Richard's Pipit	*Anthus novaeseelandiae*
Rock Pipit	*A. petrosus*
Meadow Pipit	*A. pratensis*
Swallow	*Hirundo rustica*
Yellow Wagtail	*Motacilla flava flavissima*
Grey Wagtail	*M. cinerea*
Pied Wagtail	*M. alba yarrellii*
Black Redstart	*Phoenicurus ochruros*
Redstart	*P. phoenicurus*

Whinchat	*Saxicola rubetra*
Stonechat	*S. torquata*
Wheatear	*Oenanthe oenanthe*
Fieldfare	*Turdus pilaris*
Mistle Thrush	*T. viscivorus*
Cetti's Warbler	*Cettia cetti*
Aquatic Warbler	*Acrocephalus paludicola*
Sedge Warbler	*A. schoenobaenus*
Marsh Warbler	*A. palustris*
Reed Warbler	*A. scirpaceus*
Melodious Warbler	*Hippolais polyglotta*
Dartford Warbler	*Sylvia undata*
Lesser Whitethroat	*S. curruca*
Whitethroat	*S. communis*
Garden Warbler	*S. borin*
Blackcap	*S. atricapilla*
Wood Warbler	*Phylloscopus sibilatrix*
Chiffchaff	*P. collybita*
Willow Warbler	*P. trochilus*
Firecrest	*Regulus ignicapillus*
Spotted Flycatcher	*Muscicapa striata*
Bearded Tit	*Panurus biarmicus*
Long-tailed Tit	*Aegithalos caudatus*
Coal Tit	*Parus ater*
Blue Tit	*P. caeruleus*
Great Tit	*P. major*
Short-toed Treecreeper	*Certhia brachydactyla*
Golden Oriole	*Oriolus oriolus*
Red-backed Shrike	*Lanius collurio*
Raven	*Corvus corax*
Chaffinch	*Fringilla coelebs*
Serin	*Serinus serinus*
Siskin	*Carduelis spinus*
Linnet	*C. cannabina*
Lapland Bunting	*Calcarius lapponicus*
Snow Bunting	*Plectrophenax nivalis*
Yellowhammer	*Emberiza citrinella*
Cirl Bunting	*E. cirlus*
Reed Bunting	*E. schoeniclus*